DISMANTLING
DOCTRINES
OF DEMONS

∼ VOLUME ONE ∼
DISCLOSING THE DARKNESS

RICK M. SMITH

TEMPLATES
Of Truth Publishing
A DIVISION OF SMITH PROFESSIONAL SERVICES, LLC

ACKNOWLEDGMENTS

Writing a book is the easier part. Getting it publish-ready is more difficult especially if this is your first effort. I am grateful for the many web-based resources that provide invaluable guidance and information. The two most helpful to me have been the *Self-Publishing School* team and their CEO, Chandler Bolt, who provide a staggering wealth of resources to help maneuver all the intricate steps of self-publishing & marketing online. The other is the *Jerry Jenkins Writer's Guild*. That name might ring familiar to many as the co-author with Tim LaHaye of the "Left Behind" series and best-selling author of many other books. Jerry and his experienced team provide the writer with many insights to help develop & sharpen one's writing & editing skills. *Grammarly* has been another great tool in the editing process. Without these resources, I would be lost and overwhelmed by the myriad of things one must know in getting a book in the hands of readers.

Writing a faith-based, non-fiction book filled with an abundance of Biblical interpretation & application is not a short-term project but rather one born out of our spiritual journey with God in His Word and the community of faith we have associated with over many years. I am grateful to know and serve with many trusted friends and long-term partners in ministry with whom I have shared my draft manuscripts for review. The responses they have shared have been affirming, encouraging, and their input has helped shape the direction of this publication and those that will follow. I am eternally grateful for their wise counsel and spiritual discernment.

Social media has served to connect me with a close network of many friends & acquaintances. Nearly 200 of them (too many to name) have become part of my Launch Team in the release of this first volume. Their support, encouragement, and affirming comments are most appreciated, but even more, I value the fact we share a common perspective and sense of urgency about the message in this book. They have enthusiastically climbed aboard to help promote it. Without them, this divine assignment would be greatly challenging.

The staff with which I serve at Humphrey Funeral Service in Russellville, Arkansas, provides not only a rewarding work environment but an accountability team that is most valuable. The thoughtful discussions and spiritual insights we often share affirm our common convictions, principles, and Scriptural understanding. Without their brotherhood in the faith, I would be at a certain deficit indeed.

There is a little white-frame Southern Baptist church building on the corner of Morgan Road and State Highway 124 in the Moreland community of Arkansas, frequented by a group of faithful worshippers who have extended to me the blessed privilege of being their pastor for more than a decade. They have patiently & lovingly listened to my many long sermons over the years and ministered to me and our family as much, if not more than we have ministered to them. Thank you, Moreland First Baptist Church, for being a sweet and cherished church family with which to serve, worship, learn & grow together in our faith journeys.

Certainly not least, is a loving wife and family who has lived the life of a minister's home for more than 45 years! We have literally maneuvered the best of times and the worst of times together and by the grace and mercy of the Lord we serve, always come out strengthened as a result. Their unwavering love, support, and encouragement are absolutely essential to making ministry even possible. Words cannot adequately express how much I love you and appreciate all you do to assure my emotional, physical, and spiritual health and happiness. It is much of what makes me what I am.

Thank you all from the deepest part of my heart & soul. You are all "co-authors" in this endeavor.

TABLE OF CONTENTS

The Diabolical Network of Evil

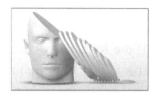

PREFACE

The embattled presidency of Donald Trump served our country in several ways, only one of which was to show the stark contrast in political ideologies shaping our partisan government. His commitment to "drain the swamp" proved, if nothing else, there is a "swamp," and the "deep state" is not just some figment of the conspiracist imagination. For the first time in our nation's history, we began to see clear indications of a real sinister presence gaining stronger footholds on state & federal policy and not at all afraid to show itself in forceful, arrogant style.

The radical shifts of Obama-era politics in legalizing same-sex marriage and advancing abortion rights remained steady despite the restraints put in place by the Trump administration. The LGBT agenda has become a militant force exerting acceptance with laws enacted to guarantee accommodation in nearly every public arena. If anyone speaks out against the homosexual lifestyle, they may even be prosecuted in some states under laws that protect LGBT persons from "hate language."

Abortion has become the new birth control to remedy the "oops" of permissive sexual freedom & expression. Many Americans were stunned when New York's abortion law (The Reproductive Health Act) was expanded in 2020 to allow some abortions after 24 weeks by even licensed midwives. The term, "after" can include right up to the time of birth "if the fetus is not viable or if the health or life of the mother is at risk." The law requires such factors must be determined by a medical practitioner, but like other medical terms, "health" and "vitality" are not defined in the New York state law leaving their application vaguely open to interpretation.[1]

The racial division revealing itself through protest riots stemming from perceptions of social injustice over the past several years reminds many of the turbulent riots of the '60s associated with the civil rights movement.

Who would have thought we would ever see the day in America when city police could be defunded; when sections of cities could be seized and come under revolutionary control; when our nation's capitol building could come under domestic attack; when pre-adolescent boys could decide they are girls and girls decide they are boys with the full support of their parents, the government, and the psychological & medical communities; when provisions under the Affordable Care Act (Obama-Care) would force our tax dollars to fund sex-change operations for transgender people; when such persons could be appointed as cabinet members in a presidential administration and be celebrated in the name of diversity, inclusion, and equal rights?

---

[1] New York State Senator Liz Krueger, *FAQs about the Reproductive Health Act,* February 12, 2019, www.nysenate.gov.

And then came COVID-19, the global pandemic that changed everything! Who would have ever thought we would live to see the day in this country when restaurants, businesses, schools, and churches would be locked down, citizens quarantined to their homes for months; and their re-openings strictly regulated by federal & state government oversight; when wearing a mask, maintaining a social distance, and taking a vaccine would be government-mandated or you could lose your job?

Like millions of others, my mind was reeling with these radical patterns developing across our national and international landscape as we approached the November 2020 elections. While attempting to rationalize what in the world was going on, my eyes caught the revealing words of the Apostle Paul in I Timothy 4:1 - *The Spirit explicitly says, in the later times some will fall away from the faith paying attention to deceitful spirits and doctrines of demons.* For me, it was one of those spiritual epiphanies, an "Ah-ha" moment in Biblical study. My focus became fixed on "doctrines of demons" and what those might be. A doctrine is a system of beliefs and practices, like our denominational beliefs as churches. What possible demonic doctrines could be permeating our culture and influencing the practice of radical evil throughout our nation and world?

My initial list was some 15-20 items long, but eventually, I dwindled them down to five fundamental doctrines. In the months leading up to the 2020 presidential election, I preached a series of sermons to the church I pastor on the subject, "Doctrines of Demons." The election was over, Biden won the White House, we got through the Holiday Season, and sometime after the first of the new year, I decided to go back and revisit this study. I dug a little deeper, broadened my research, expanded my notes, and started writing. I didn't intentionally set out to write a book, but it became evident early in the process that a book would be the outcome. It also became apparent that this was an assignment divinely inspired and providentially ordered by the Lord.

Nearly a year later, the manuscript was completed. Being the long-winded preacher I tend to be, the first draft was over 500 pages. Several of my close confidants to whom I shared the manuscript for review encouraged me to break the book apart into several volumes for fear readers might not be inclined to engage a 500-page book. They were of the firm opinion the book was too timely and pertinent to miss the opportunity for as many as possible to be reached through its message.

After careful evaluation, I decided to release *Dismantling Doctrines of Demons* into three separate volumes, the first of which is this release - *Disclosing the Darkness.* Subsequent volumes will address *Defining the Doctrines* and *Discovering the Deliverance.* We cannot understand the effects of the doctrines without first gaining a clear perspective of the system of darkness driving them; and for those who might find themselves encumbered in these strongholds of evil, the way of deliverance is essential to discover and experience.

The idea there might actually be demonic spirits engaging our culture, government, and domestic life seems laughingly superstitious, science-fictional, or Hollywood horror flick fascination for many today. Jesus confronted and delivered various persons from demonic possession throughout His earthly ministry. He even spoke directly to those demons, and they talked back! Paul,

James, Luke, Matthew, Mark, Jude, and John all address the subject of demons in their respective New Testament writings. They are mentioned in Old Testament accounts by several of the prophets. Despite the casual, even entertaining approach to their reality by modern society, demonic beings, and satanic powers do exist today and are gaining active momentum as the world moves deeper into end-time events. While outward manifestations of their presence might not often be observed, this book focuses more on their covert operations, which amazingly escape the awareness of many in our nation and world.

I have remained firmly committed to a serious & scholarly study of the Scriptures through the years. Paramount in the development of this book has been my deep conviction & commitment to assure Biblical integrity, accuracy, proper interpretation, and application be solidly maintained throughout. While your understanding and interpretation of specific Scriptural passages may differ from some of the positions I have presented, I hope there is enough common ground in our understanding of faith to guard those differences against becoming a litmus test of our spiritual fellowship and ability to learn from one another.

Early in my Biblical studies, I discovered that keen attention must be paid to the original languages of the Old Testament Hebrew and New Testament Greek writings to assure proper interpretation & application of the Scripture. I discovered what many scholars assert in the New American Standard Version (NASV) as one of the most accurate translations to the earliest manuscripts. For these reasons, the NASV became my choice of study early in life and is used most often throughout the Scriptural quotations in this book.

Like all preachers & teachers, you might note my use of some repetitive phrases. For instance, "God's Word, will, and ways." I use this phrase often to draw emphasis to the inspiration & authority of Scripture; the importance of living out the will, plan & purpose of God for each of our lives; and the faithfulness & obedience required of us to bask in the blessings of His glory, goodness, and greatness. Therein lies yet another common characteristic of my presentations – three "G's" or four "P's," etc. I find this approach is helpful in the effective retention of teaching points. Portions of Biblical text which relate to the theme & purpose of this writing are also replicated each time an additional point or insight is gleaned from them. I hope you don't find the repetition too distracting.

One more final point before we begin this journey together. Paul teaches us the *Holy Spirit searches all things, even the depths of God...the thoughts of God* (I Corinthians 2:10-12). Affirming the teaching of Jesus indicating the Holy Spirit will *take of Mine and disclose to you* (John 16:14), Paul goes on to say the Holy Spirit enables us to *know the things freely given to us by God, which things we also speak, not in words taught by human wisdom, but in those taught by the Spirit, combining spiritual thoughts with spiritual words* (2:12-13).

This revelation holds significant value to me. It reminds me of the words of Solomon when he wrote - *In addition to being a wise man, the Preacher also taught the people knowledge; and he pondered, searched out, and arranged many proverbs. The Preacher sought to find delightful words and to write words of truth correctly. The words of wise men are like goads, and masters of these collections are like well-driven nails; they are given by one Shepherd. But beyond this, my son, be warned: the writing of many books is endless, and excessive devotion to books is wearying to the body. The conclusion, when all has been heard, is: fear God and keep His commandments because this applies to every person. For God will bring every act to judgment, everything which is hidden, whether it is good or evil* (Ecclesiastes 12:9-14). This has been a guiding force in my effort of writing. Every word throughout has been consistently prayed over with an earnest desire for God to anoint my words and thoughts to convey His words and thoughts accurately & effectively. I encourage you to read them with this sincere and confident aspiration & accountability in mind.

By focusing this book on the system, strategies, and schemes of darkness, I do not want to leave the impression we are facing an insurmountable enemy. Satan is defeated, it is already decreed by the God of Heaven. Still, we are in a spiritual battle the church has become complacent about and far too comfortable with. One of my purposes is to wake the people of God up to the reality war is raging around us and we are called to the battlefield. We go, however, with the clear understanding that we will conquer because *greater is He who is in you than he who is in the world* (I John 4:4); and, *the Lord your God who goes before you will Himself fight on your behalf* (Deuteronomy 1:30). So, fear not my friends, we win!

Are you ready? Let's begin our understanding together of *Dismantling Doctrines of Demons* by first gaining a clear knowledge of the diabolical system of evil driving these doctrines as we *Disclose the Darkness.*

Blessings,
Rick Smith

INTRODUCTION

The Apostle Paul preached the Gospel across ancient Asia Minor for some 30 years. By the time he wrote his first letter to young Timothy, his colleague in ministry, Paul had just been released from being under house arrest in Rome for almost two years. He must have felt some sense his life would soon be ending because his expressions of revelation and urgency carry a certain intensity throughout. The second of these two letters is held as the last words dictated in Scripture from the great Apostle. Swan songs tend to carry significant value and special significance, and these letters to Timothy bear those marks. Among those final expressions are these sobering words:

> *But the Spirit explicitly says that in the later times, some will fall away from the faith, paying attention to deceitful spirits and doctrines of demons* (I Timothy 4:1).

Do you feel a certain uneasiness when you read those words? They reveal a mysterious & sinister presence coming, so powerful and convincing some will defect from their faith and follow deceptive ideologies. Paul declares this presence, and these ideologies originate in a supernatural underworld of darkness and evil, an invisible principality where Satan and demonic forces thrive. They hold the power to access our visible reality and influence the thoughts & activities of people and societies to accomplish their evil intent. Note the five perspectives in this short but impacting statement:

Source – Paul reveals his source of revelation as being directly from the *Holy Spirit*.

Season – the evidence of this sobering condition will become more and more apparent during the days of the final dispensation or the *later times* of the church age.

Separation – this time will be marked by a stark shift in belief patterns. Some will begin *paying attention to* what is systematically false and abandon what was before held sacredly true, resulting in a strategic *falling away from the faith*.

Surrogates – those who will facilitate this radical shift will be *deceitful spirits*.

Standard – the standard to which this shift turns will be a system & strategy of darkness described as *doctrines of demons*.

Let's expand these five sections a bit more to gain the full impact of Paul's revelation:

SOURCE – The Spirit Explicitly Says:

Paul is assuring us his source of information is not his human intelligence, personal opinion, or formative perspectives on the matter; it is not from the political environment of his day or any popular assertion within his ancient culture. Paul is declaring the sole source of this insight comes as divine revelation directly from *the Holy Spirit*.

This should not be surprising, since Jesus taught us one of the roles of the Holy Spirit would be to – *guide you into all truth; for He will not speak of His own initiative, but whatever He hears, He will speak; and He will disclose to you what is to come* (John 16:13). The Holy Spirit, who indwells every true believer in Christ, speaks on behalf of the Father; and, what He hears from the Father, He declares to us. Among the many things the Holy Spirit reveals to us, He discloses – *what is to come.*

It is interesting to note how teaching on Biblical prophecy has evolved over the years. When I was a teenager, Hal Lindsey published two bestsellers, *The Late Great Planet Earth* (Zondervan, 1970) and *There's a New World Coming* (Vision House, 1973). Prophecy teaching went abuzz across the evangelical community in countless sermon series, tape series, books, articles, television & radio broadcasts, etc. It seemed no matter what the preacher chose as his sermon text & theme, somehow it always circled back to the topic of prophecy. Eventually, the church grew weary on any subject relative to eschatology (the study of the end times). The lull which followed surged to revival once again in the mid-1990s with the publication by Tim LaHaye & Jerry Jenkins of the *Left Behind* series, reportedly selling close to 80 million copies![2]

This up-and-down pattern of prophetic teaching seems to have characterized the past 50 years. Depending on where you look across the Christian landscape, you will find pastors, preachers & teachers with a strong passion for prophetic teaching, others who touch upon it from time to time, and still others who leave the subject entirely to everyone else. The arena of prophetic teachers includes too many who tend to sensationalize Scriptural references to ideas & conclusions way beyond the context and apply them to current world events in ways many consider too questionable for responsible Biblical scholarship. Still, others simply throw up their hands and forget it, exhausted from their efforts to figure out all the confusing & challenging symbolisms involved.

But despite this vacillation in handling eschatological theology, one cannot get past the mere fact the Holy Spirit discloses to us things that are *to come*. According to *The Encyclopedia of Biblical Prophecy* by J. Barton Payne, there are 1,239 prophecies in the Old Testament and 578 prophecies in the New Testament for a total of 1,817. These prophecies are contained in 8,352 of the Bible's verses. Since there are 31,124 verses in the Bible, the 8,352 verses containing prophecy constitute 26.8 percent of the Bible's volume.[3] While many have already been historically fulfilled, many have yet to come to pass.

---

[2] Camila Domonoske, Tim LaHaye, Evangelical Legend Behind "Left Behind" Series, Dies at 90, July 25, 2016, www.npr.org.

[3] Dr. J. Barton Payne, *Encyclopedia of Biblical Prophecy: The Complete Guide to Scriptural Predictions and Their Fulfillment,* 1973, Wipf and Stock Publishers, Eugene, Oregon.

If we accurately handle *the word of truth* (II Timothy 2:15), we cannot escape our responsibility to teach what the *inspired* Word says (II Timothy 3:16) about prophecy. As best we can, we must have a good understanding of *what is to come*, and the Holy Spirit is our most reliable source of information, just as He was Paul's.

That the Holy Spirit *explicitly says* raises yet two additional perspectives:

Utterance

The Greek word means to speak with obvious, distinct, and precise words. Did Paul hear an audible voice he understood was the Holy Spirit? I don't think we can discount such a possibility. In Paul's conversion experience on the road to Damascus, Luke reports – *suddenly a light from heaven flashed around him, and he fell to the ground and heard a voice saying to him, "Saul, Saul, why are you persecuting Me?" And he said, "Who are You, Lord?" And He said, "I am Jesus whom you are persecuting."* (Acts 9:3-4). Biblical history is filled with numerous examples of God's people hearing God's voice guiding them in God's work. Paul's experience is certainly no different. The Greek word *heard* refers to audible sound coming to the spiritual heart through physical ears.

Do people hear the audible voice of heaven today? Most of us have heard someone say they have, and I would dare not say they have not. God deals with each of us in unique ways, and if it serves His purpose with any particular person to reveal Himself in audible ways, it indeed rests within the power of God to do so.

I would also note in the ancient times in which Paul lived, we have one thing he did not – the complete volume of Scripture. The Bible is God's written revelation of Himself to man. If we want to hear from God, all we need do is search the Scriptures because God most often speaks to us through the pages of His Word – *All Scripture is inspired by God and profitable for teaching, for reproof, for correction, for training in righteousness; that the man of God may be adequate, equipped for every good work* (II Timothy 3:16-17). The Psalmist knew the source of God's voice of wisdom and prayed, *Open my eyes, that I may behold wonderful things from Thy law* (Psalm 119:18).

Before Scripture was complete, God revealed words of truth to His people in various ways, including angels, dreams, visions, tongues, and prophecy. However, Paul tells us many of these mediums will reach a point of having served their purpose and will no longer be needed – *if there are gifts of prophecy, they will be done away; if there are tongues, they will cease; if there is knowledge, it will be done away. For we know in part, and we prophesy in part; but when the perfect comes, the partial will be done away* (I Corinthians 13:8-10). The Greek word translated *perfect* means complete. The word translated *done away* means to abolish or cease.

To what is Paul referring when he deems it *perfect*? There is no more complete perfection than what awaits us in God's presence in heaven. All our human resources and modes of communication utilized in this present world will have little purpose or value there. We will – *know fully just as we have been fully known* (I Corinthians 13:12). But is it possible Paul's insight may also be interpreted to include an interim instrument of perfection given to help bridge the gap between this life and our eternal destiny of perfection to come? Is it possible Paul may be referring to completed Scripture - the Bible?

Dr. John Phillips supports this suggestion – "Until the New Testament canon was complete, nobody had access to the full and final revelation."[4] Dr. Warren Wiersbe shares a similar view – "In the New Testament (which at the time was not completed), we have a complete revelation, but our understanding of it is partial."[5]

Dr. W.A. Criswell, in preaching this text at Dallas First Baptist Church, asserts the same – "What need we now of a man who says, 'I have a revelation from God,' when the whole fullness of God's revelation is here in the Book I hold in my hand! What of use when a man says, 'I have the gift of knowledge,' and he stands up and he judges between this prophecy and this prophecy as to which one is pertinent for us now when I have the complete, the TELEIOS, the consummation, the mature, the whole revelation of God here in the Book? He is not needed, he is not needed; they belong to the infancy of the church when we didn't have the Bible, and the people gathered together knew not what to do. But the part is now swallowed up in the whole."[6]

The great Christian scientist, Dr. Henry Morris, Sr. agrees – "'That which is perfect' cannot refer to Christ at His second coming, for 'that' is a neuter pronoun. Since the previous verse refers to the

---

[4] Dr. John Phillips, *The John Phillips Commentary Series: Exploring I Corinthians,* page 299, 2002, Kregel Publications, Grand Rapids, Michigan.

[5] Dr. Warren Wiersbe, *The Bible Exposition Commentary, New Testament Volume 1,* page 611, 2001, Victor, Colorado Springs, Colorado.

[6] Dr. W.A. Criswell, *The More Excellent Way,* December 4, 1955, First Baptist Church, Dallas, Texas, audio sermon, www.wacriswell.com.

incompleteness of the divine revelation at that time, 'that which is perfect (that is, complete) almost certainly refers to the completion of Biblical revelation, as finally announced by John, the last of the apostles (Revelation 22:18-19). We now have all the prophetic truth needed in the Scriptures for the guidance of the church until Christ comes again. With few, if any, exceptions, we also have all the attestation we need to its veracity and power, so there is little need anymore for miraculous signs, even though many still desire them."[7]

While it remains a matter of differing interpretation among Bible students, many agree with this formidable application. There is room in the original grammar and the broader context to allow this distinguishing interpretation.

Here is my point – I cannot trust the word of a mere man who claims to have heard the voice of God in a dream or a vision giving him a revelation of something purportedly to come. In the days following the 2020 Presidential election, YouTube was replete with "prophets" predicting exact days when the election of Joe Biden would be overturned, and Donald Trump would continue to serve as our President. Those dates came and went, and Joe Biden maintained his occupancy of the Oval Office at the White House. So, where is the integrity and reliability of their proclaimed prophetic visions?

While I can never place my complete confidence in the words of man, I can ALWAYS trust the Word of God! I never have to guess whether God's Word contains His absolute, inerrant, infallible, and inspired truth. It does, and it is! I can trust its history, prophecies,

---

[7] Dr. Henry M. Morris, *The New Defender's Study Bible,* 2006, Word Publishing, Nashville, Tennessee.

commands, precepts, and the vast knowledge, wisdom, & understanding it gives me about God and spiritual things. We have in completed form what the ancients only had in partiality – God's written Word, the Bible. It is God's voice speaking to man.

Urgency

In addition, the idea of the Greek word *explicitly* seems to be a matter of exclusive urgency. It would be like me to say, "I have something significant I need to tell you, and I do not want to call you, email you, or text you. This is something we need to discuss in person as soon as possible." What the Holy Spirit is about to reveal to the Apostle Paul is a matter of spiritual urgency & importance that will have a significant impact on the Church Age. We must listen up and take heed!

I have taken the time to emphasize this point because it is essential to understand this revelation is a direct quote from the God of heaven. It is not something we should doubt or question. We can accept it as absolute God-spoken truth. This revelation addresses the presence of *deceitful spirits* and the practice of *demonic doctrines*. As sensational as many in our world today would think the idea of *spirits* and *demons* to be, this is real!

SEASON – That in the Later Times:

Having understood the source of our revelation, we move to the question of when this revealed truth will come to pass. Through Paul, the Holy Spirit *explicitly* tells us it will be – *in the later times.* Two primary Greek words qualify time in the New Testament - KAIROS and CHRONOS. The latter refers to chronological time, such as hours, minutes, days, weeks, months, and years. The first word, KAIROS, is the word Paul uses here, and it refers to an undefined period that is proper or ripe with opportunity.

Although our calendar designates the first day of Spring, the season we experience as Spring has no set number of days it endures. We know it is Spring when the temperature warms, the grass begins to green, and buds break out on branches. Some years we might experience a longer Spring and a shorter one in other years.

An *American Idol* judge said to one of the contestants, "This is your time," referring to the opportunity for success & stardom encasing the moment for them. When leaving a particular job, we might say to ourselves, "It's just time to move on." These examples qualify a time right and rich with opportunity, yet undefined in terms of hours, days, or years. These are examples of KAIROS time.

The Holy Spirit further reveals this time is during a *later* period of the season God has designated to fulfill His prophetic plan and purpose. Paul uses a similar designation when he says – *in the last days, difficult times will come* (II Timothy 3:1). KAIROS refers to the season of *difficulty*, while ESCHATOS refers to this season's last or latter portion.

From this Greek word, ESCHATOS comes our English word, Eschatology, which is the theological study of prophecy and the end times. So, the phrase, *later times* refers to a season when eschatological and prophetic events unfold as God established them to be in His Word. We are in the eschatological season often referred to as the Church Age. It began when Jesus ascended into heaven

(Acts 1:9-11) and will end at the prophetic event commonly identified as the Rapture of the Church (I Thessalonians 4:13-18).

Even though the Church Age began at a specific past event in history and will end with a particular future event, it otherwise has no defined period. We do not know how many days or years are set between these two historical events. In fact – *It is not for you to know times* (CHRONOS) *or epochs* (KAIROS) *which the Father has fixed by His own authority* (Acts 1:7). All the timeframes for the eschatological periods in the Bible are known only by God. Jesus affirmed – *no one knows, not even the angels of heaven, nor the Son, but the Father alone* (Matthew 24:36). Those who have attempted to pinpoint a predicted date have only suffered scorn and embarrassment from their failed attempts.

Two time-related conditions do, however, provide indications of when we are living in the *later times*:

Displays

When we look around us and take note of world conditions, we see many things on display alerting us to the times in which we live. The disciples once asked Jesus – *Tell us…what will be the sign of Your coming, and of the end of the age?* (Matthew 24:3). His answer reveals many things being on display, such as false prophets, wars, famines, earthquakes, tribulation, apostasy, abominations, and atmospheric & celestial phenomena.

Then Jesus said – *Learn the parable from the fig tree: when its branch has already become tender and puts forth its leaves, you know that summer is near; even so, you too, when you see all these things, recognize that He is near, right at the door* (Matthew 24:32-33). Imagine a visitor coming to your house. He has pulled into your driveway, exited his vehicle, climbed your steps, walked across your front porch, and is now *right at the door* with his armed raised, ready to knock. Jesus describes the things on display that will alert us when we are living during the *later times* when He is *right at the door*. Much of what Jesus describes is on grand display even today.

Dispensations

"Dispensational Pre-millennialism" is a fancy theological term defining specific views in Biblical eschatology. Without getting into all the intricate details which qualify this view, fundamentally, it includes the idea that across the course of KAIROS (time), more and more, bit by bit, God's prophetic program is being revealed.

We have noted three things Paul has identified as characterizing the later times: the presence of *deceitful spirits,* the practice of *doctrines of demons,* and the increasing progression of *difficult times* (I Timothy 4:1; II Timothy 3:1). His expanded list that follows includes – *men will be lovers of self, lovers of money, boastful, arrogant, revilers, disobedient to parents, ungrateful, unholy, unloving, irreconcilable, malicious gossips, without self-control, brutal, haters of good, treacherous, reckless, conceited, lovers of pleasure rather than lovers of God; holding to a form of godliness, although they have denied its power* (II Timothy 3:2-5). Are we to think all these things were not present in the ancient culture in which Paul lived and wrote these words (A.D. 64-67)? They were indeed.

The basic dynamic behind the dispensational view holds that these things are revealed more and more as we move across the course of time, and their frequency and severity increase as we move closer to the last days of the *later times*. The world groans for peace and diplomacy, and much effort is expended to bring about peace. While that is good, and we certainly should try, the Christian must always house those efforts within the context of Jesus' dispensational prophecy – *lawlessness (will) increase* (Matthew 24:12). Paul affirmed – *evil men and imposters will proceed from bad to worse, deceiving and being deceived* (II Timothy 3:13).

I like to illustrate this dispensational dynamic using a picture puzzle. The front of the box presents an image of the finished puzzle once all the 1,000 or so pieces are joined together. As you work the puzzle, fewer and fewer pieces remain on the table. With fewer pieces remaining, the pace with which you work the puzzle picks up. When the last few dozen pieces remain, seeing where they fit and moving them into place is very quick & easy. This progression serves as a good analogy for describing the dispensational dynamic at work in the cadence of the *later times*. More recently, it has been referred to as "prophetic acceleration" or "prophetic compression."

What Paul saw happening in his day is happening with even greater frequency and intensity in our day. It will grow even more prevalent in the days to come until it reaches a critical crescendo at the time of the Rapture of the Church. Accordingly, we are in the season of time ripe for Paul's revelation in I Timothy 4:1 to manifest itself.

We have considered the source and the season of this revealing prophecy. Let's move on to a sobering condition it discloses.

SEPARATION – Some Will Fall Away from the Faith:

What purpose do *doctrines of demons* and the work of *deceitful spirits* serve to accomplish? Of the many possibilities, one is specifically to drive *some* to *fall away from the faith*.

There are two spiritual classifications of persons who are Satan's targets. The first is the lost man. An evangelist once said, "Why should the devil waste his time on a lost man? He already has him. He just needs to work a little to keep him," and he does! The second classification is those who associate with God. Satan hates God, God's people, and God's church. He will do everything he can to wreak havoc in the lives of God's people because of his tremendous wrath toward God. Seeing people *fall away from the faith* causes the greatest celebrations throughout the caverns of hell.

Like many in the evangelical community, this writer holds strongly to the doctrine commonly referred to as the "Security of the Believer," which I think can be most effectively defended Biblically. The *falling away* phenomenon in Paul's prophecy stirs up many sobering concerns we must make sure we sort through and understand before moving forward.

First, we must define who Paul refers to when he identifies *some*. The Greek word refers to certain & various ones; not everyone, but some (an undefined number).

We must also keep in mind Paul's audience. He was writing to Timothy, who was pastor at the time (about A.D. 62) at the church in ancient Ephesus. Such New Testament letters were commonly meant to be shared with those within the church, so Paul's audience would have been a group of believers who served & worshipped with Timothy at Ephesus. Many such letters were circulatory, meaning they were read in other area churches as well. Since this letter became incorporated into the canon of inspired Scripture, we accept Paul's writing as universally applying throughout history to the church at large, even to our modern time. So, *some* refers to those who associate at least in some way with faith & belief about Christ.

Secondly, we must define what it means to *fall away from the faith*. The Greek word translated *fall away* is where we get our English word "apostasy." It means to depart from, desert, leave or withdraw from. It is similar to when a person might leave America, travel to Russia, and denounce his United States citizenship to defect to that foreign government. The Scriptural context here is not a nationality to which Paul connects the apostasy, but rather a *faith*. Obviously, Paul is referring to a spiritual faith specifically related to God and the things of God.

As disconcerting as it is, the apparent truth from this prophetic revelation as given to Paul *explicitly by the Holy Spirit* declares that in the *later times* an undefined number of individuals who have previously associated themselves with the tenants of the Christian faith will come to abandon those beliefs. They will depart from their affiliation with and withdraw from their accommodation of any previous belief about God. They will defect from the faith.

This raises some serious and uncomfortable questions: How could a genuine, born-again believer in Christ make such a decision? How could a long-time follower of Christ ever reach that kind of resolve? Is Paul talking about various Christians who will one day lose their salvation? Is it possible for a true believer in Christ to lose his salvation?

Let's attempt to answer the most serious of those questions – Is it possible for a true believer in Christ to lose his salvation? Some church denominations and doctrinal belief systems teach this possibility as very real. This writer is not among them. I am one of those good old Southern Baptist boys who adopt the "once saved, always saved" position on the question. It is not because of how I was raised in the church, but instead because I have carefully studied the Scriptures and have confidently concluded the Bible strategically defends a secure relationship with God through Jesus Christ.

Allow me to summarize this defense from five perspectives:

The Promise

In telling Nicodemus, *unless one is born again, he cannot see the kingdom of God* (John 3:3), Jesus promised, *whoever believes may in Him have eternal life* (3:15); followed by an oft-quoted promise of Scripture – *For God so loved the world, that He gave His only begotten Son, that whoever believes in Him should not perish, but have eternal life* (John 3:26). Jesus promised on another occasion – *the one who comes to Me, I will certainly not cast out* (John 6:37). Paul affirmed – *whoever will call upon the name of the Lord will be saved* (Romans 10:13). The promise could not be any more explicit. When we are truly born-again, we attain the gift of eternal life with God in heaven. The very word *eternal* means never ceasing. It is a secure state of spiritual perpetuity.

However, this promise needs further qualification because a person cannot claim to be a Christian and live any way he chooses while still expecting to go to heaven, as critics of the "once saved, always saved" position insist. They are right. A careful explanation of one Greek word used in these verses will help us tremendously in settling this objection – the word PISTEWO, which translated means "faith."

This word poses a translational issue between the Greek and English languages. PISTEWO (faith) is both a noun and a verb in the Greek language. In the English language, *faith* is only a noun or noun derivative. We do not know the word faith as an action word. When was the last time you went out faithing? Or, when you said to your spouse, "I faith you?" You get the point.

When King James (I) desired to give the English people the benefit of Holy Scripture to read & study, he empaneled a stately group of 47 scholars & theologians and assigned them the critical task of translating the Old Testament Hebrew and New Testament Greek manuscripts into the English language. In 1611, they completed their assignment and issued the first edition of what we have today as the King James Version of the Bible.

You can imagine what an extensive task this must have been. Many Hebrew & Greek words presented varying degrees of challenge, but none greater than the Greek word PISTEWO. They searched throughout the English language for a transliteration of the word, but the only word they could find which came anywhere close to the meaning of PISTEWO was the word, *believe*. Accordingly, the Greek text was rendered – *whoever PISTEWO [faiths] believes in Him should not perish but have eternal life* (John 3:16). The problem remained, however, that *believe* did not convey all the rich meanings of PISTEWO.

While attending a Bible Conference at Quachita Baptist University in 1978, I heard the late Dr. Jack McGorman (1920-2021) of Southwestern Baptist Seminary in Fort Worth, Texas, explain this unique Greek word. It has three essential elements:

First is the element of **belief.** To be born-again (saved), we certainly must believe in Jesus Christ. He is not just a name on numerous pages of a best-selling book; He is a real person who lived during human history. During that time, He proclaimed Himself to be the Son of God and the promised Messiah, sent to redeem humanity from the penalty of sin (death), making a way possible for a man to be reconciled spiritually back to God since that fellowship was severed by the fall of man in the Garden.

If a person does not believe these essential things about Jesus Christ, he cannot be saved. We must believe Jesus is who He proclaimed Himself to be, that He loves us, has the power & willingness to forgive all our sin; and, if we believe in Him, He will impart to us the gift of eternal life with God in heaven. Jesus died on a cross for the sins of the world. He came back to life from the grave. He ascended back into heaven, and He is coming back to earth again. We must believe all these things.

But is it enough simply to believe these things? Apparently not, because James reveals *the demons also believe and shudder* (James 2:19). There is not a demon in hell who does not know exactly who Jesus is and much of what He has accomplished in God's eternal plan. The demons of hell know & believe more about Jesus, God, and heaven than many people do! Demons have no place in heaven, however. Their destiny is hell which has *been prepared for the devil and his demons* (Matthew 25:41). So, if belief alone is no ticket for demons into heaven, it holds no guarantee for you and me, either. It is, however, one of three essential elements for salvation. The devil and his demons would never agree to the following two, even if they could.

The second element is **commitment.** A person must commit his or her life to Jesus Christ based on their beliefs about Him. I can observe a chair and say I believe it is made of material strong enough and constructed in a way sturdy enough to hold me up if I were to sit in it. If we go no further, I have only told you what I believe about the chair. It is not until I sit in the chair that I prove to you it will do what I believe it can do. I make a commitment to the chair based on what I believe about it.

Let's look at it from another illustration we find in Scripture. Our relationship with God is often pictured in the relationship of marriage. In the New Testament, the church is pictured as the Bride of Christ, and Jesus as our Bridegroom. When Paul quoted the Old Testament passage where God instituted the relationship of marriage, *For this cause a man shall leave his father and mother, and shall cleave to his wife; and the two shall become one flesh* (Ephesians 5:32; Genesis 2:24), he added this interesting suffix – *this mystery is great, but I am speaking with reference to Christ and the church* (Ephesians 5:32). Throughout verses 21-33, Paul has presented the roles & functions of husbands and wives as illustrated in the context of Christ and the church – *husbands, love your wives just as Christ also loved the church and gave Himself up for her*

(5:25); *wives, be subject to your own husbands, as to the Lord* (5:22). The comparison is deep with meaning.

Now let's put this meaning into the element of commitment. When a man and woman first meet, there is usually an instant attraction. They desire to spend more time together getting to know each other. Their affections grow into deeper emotions of love as they experience courtship life together. As their relationship grows, they move to a point where they want to spend the rest of their lives together and become engaged.

That decision is based on what they believe about each other. They believe each of them has all the relational qualities necessary to make one another happy in life. She believes he will make a good provider, protect her, take care of her, and make a great father one day. He believes she is gorgeous, fun, intelligent, and creative. He believes she will be an excellent companion with him throughout life. They both cannot imagine life without each other.

If these affirmations of belief are as far as this couple goes, they will never be married. They will remain in a perpetual state of courtship and engagement. They may even move in together like many cohabitating couples do today thinking some trial run will better position them for marriage when all it really amounts to is playing the marriage game without the sacrifice of commitment. That's how many people today flirt with God and keep an open option for easy exit should the sacrifice of Christian living require more than they are willing to invest.

This couple will not become husband & wife until they stand before family and friends in some official ceremony and publicly & legally commit their lives to one another in marriage. They make a commitment of their life to each other, based on what they believe about each other, by saying, "I do." The date is on the calendar, the big event takes place, and they celebrate that day of commitment each year as their wedding anniversary.

I remember the day I said to Jesus Christ, "I do." It was during the second week of a two-week revival meeting at my home church, Range Hills Baptist Church in Memphis, Tennessee. Yes, we really did hold two-week revivals in those days, and two-week Vacation Bible Schools as well. The fast-tract approach of most churches today just cannot imagine that! I'm eternally grateful for that second week of meetings because, on September 11, 1963, the Holy Spirit graciously moved with conviction onto the heart of this little 8-year-old boy and made me aware of my need for Jesus Christ to be my personal Savior & Lord. I walked the aisle that night and gave my heart to Him, following His example a few weeks later in believer's baptism.

When celebrating a family member or friend's birthday, my late father-in-law, Dick Markussen, would always add a second verse to the birthday song – "Happy birthday, yes two; only one will not do; born-again means salvation; how many have you?" The lyrics make you stop and think about the literality of Jesus' words to Nicodemus – *"That which is born of the flesh is flesh, and that which is born of the Spirit is spirit. Do not marvel that I said to you, 'You must be born again.'"* (John 3:6-7). Yes, two; only one will not do! So, every year on January 11, I celebrate my first (physical) birthday. Then on September 11, I celebrate my born-again (spiritual) birthday, or, as we have illustrated, my spiritual wedding anniversary.

Do you remember the time and place you said to Jesus, "I do?" The moment when you bowed your heart in love & humility and committed your life to Him as your personal Savior & Lord? Birth is an event. A wedding ceremony is an event. Both have a designated date and time on the calendar. You may not be able to remember the specific date & time of your commitment to the Lord Jesus, but you certainly should be able to remember the experience vividly in your mind and heart.

Where is the time & place when you and Jesus nailed it down? For me, it was in that Baptist revival meeting. For one of my sons, it was privately and alone in his bed one night. One of my friends was on his front porch with two men from a local church. For a teenager in my youth group, it was 3 o'clock in the morning in an overgrown, abandoned putt-putt golf course. For Saul, it was on the road to Damascus (Acts 9). Throughout your walk with God, you will often go back in your mind & heart to that day of personal commitment. Pause a moment and recall in your mind that important time & place.

We are defining three essential elements embedded in the rich meaning of the Greek word PISTEWO (faith). Belief is the first. Commitment is the second, but there is an essential third, and it is a **lifestyle.** Paul said - *Therefore if anyone is in Christ, he is a new creature; the old things passed away; behold, new things have come* (II Corinthians 5:17). In this trilogy of meaning, a commitment is made based on your belief, and then a lifestyle emerges that demonstrates or bears evidence of your commitment. Jesus said – *you will know them by their fruits* (Matthew 7:16,20).

When a man and woman commit their lives to one another in marriage, they leave a former single life behind and begin a new life together. They change directions in life. They no longer exercise the freedom to date other people and pursue other love relationships. They are now focused on building their new lives together and making their own home & family as a couple.

The design God instituted for marriage involves acts of *leaving* and *cleaving* (Genesis 2:24). The Hebrew word *leaving* means to forsake and abandon a former lifestyle, in favor of the Hebrew *cleaving* which means to be permanently glued together. This kind of Biblical commitment is almost a lost concept in our modern view of marriage. Too many couples enter a marital relationship with the idea in the back of their minds that if things don't work out, divorce is always a suitable option. There is no perspective about permanency in marriage, or as Jesus declared, *they are no longer two, but one flesh. What therefore God has joined together, let no man separate* (Matthew 19:6). Permanency in marriage symbolizes the security of the believer as we have defined it. If marriage reflects our sure & steadfast relationship with God, who promises never to divorce us, we should uphold the same enduring commitment to one another in marriage. Biblical marriage is one man for one woman for life. The lifestyles they each leave in favor of the one they begin together constitute a new lifestyle uniquely theirs.

This change in direction, behavior, choices, and lifestyle in the spiritual relationship is what we call repentance. Just as a couple abandons their former single lifestyle to commit themselves to one another in creating their marital lifestyle, a person leaves his former lifestyle of sinful choices & behaviors to live out his new relationship of following God's Word, will, and ways. This new lifestyle bears evidence of a new commitment of belief in Jesus Christ.

We cannot over-emphasize this point because it is crucial in understanding the essential dynamics of the Christian faith. It also helps us better understand how *falling away from the faith* is possible.

Suppose this husband, now newly married, had the mindset nothing changes. He can still run around with his cronies, see other women, stay gone for hours or days with no accountability to anyone but himself, make decisions on his own; pretty much everything he did when he was single. He has the best of both worlds. He can still live like he always lived, but now he has the luxury of a house, a woman to come home to, someone to cook his meals, wash his clothes, look after his kids, and throw in a second income to pay the bills and buy his toys. How long do you suppose his new wife would tolerate such a marital arrangement? If she is a sane functioning woman with any genuine self-respect, not for long!

Here is the point. Many people claim to be Christians. If you ask them, they will boldly declare they believe in Christ. They accept the Bible as the Word of God. They may even attend church on some regular basis, but they have never really made a personal commitment of their life to Jesus Christ based on what they believe about Him. Therefore, their lifestyle shows no real change in choices and behavior. No sense of repentance characterizes their claim to being a Christian. They look and act otherwise – *according to the course of this world...sons of disobedience* (Ephesians 2:2).

It is easy to fall away from something you were never really committed to in the first place or abandon a belief about something or someone you were never really surrendered to. To say, "I believe in Jesus Christ," in the New Testament way of PISTEWO, is to say, "I believe in Jesus Christ, I have committed my heart & life to Jesus Christ, and I am determined to live every moment of every day in complete obedience to God's Word, will and ways." When we are genuinely & sincerely born-again in this Biblical way, we change! Our appearance changes, language & conversations change, where we go changes, who we hang out with changes, what we do changes – *old things have passed away and new things have come.* We are a different person – *a new creature.* Our new life in Christ is made manifest in how we live, and it is a lifestyle others can see – *you will be known by your fruit.*

When you look at your life, do you see that kind of difference? Two qualities will help you know the genuineness of your claim to Christ – desire and determination. The Holy Spirit of God places a desire in your heart to live according to God's Word, will, and ways. That desire motivates you in your determination to live holy and righteous as best you can. Your life permeates with a sincere desire & determination to follow Peter's admonition – *As obedient children, do not be conformed to the former lusts which were yours in your ignorance, but like the Holy One who called you, be holy yourselves also in your behavior; because it is written, "You shall be holy, for I am holy."* (I Peter 1:14-16). If your life lacks this genuine desire and determination, I compel you to seek God for a divine introspection of your heart in helping you to know whether or not you truly belong to Him in real faith.

Let me track us back in. We are qualifying the "security of the believer" (once saved, always saved) and how this truth is vigorously defended from five Biblical perspectives. We have looked at it from the perspective of the promise. When we are genuinely born-again, our new life in Christ is perpetual and eternally secure. Jesus declares it as a divine promise.

The Proclamation

Concerning those who have genuinely committed their lives to Jesus Christ as their personal Savior & Lord, Jesus said – *I give eternal life to them, and they shall never perish; and no one shall snatch them out of My hand. My Father, who has given them to Me, is greater than all; and no one is able to snatch them out of the Father's hand. I and the Father are one* (John 10:28-30). What a glorious proclamation and affirmation! Talk about security! Isn't it a great thing to know with complete confidence & assurance that when we are genuinely born-again in Christ, He holds us firmly in His grasp, and no power on earth can pluck us out or snatch us away?!

The Prayer

Have you ever had someone say to you, "I'll be praying for you," and you wondered if you & your need even entered their mind again? How often have you and I told someone we would pray for them and never given it another thought? It is our unpredictable human nature failing us.

Jesus never fails us. When Jesus ascended into heaven (Acts 1:9-11), He was enthroned at the right hand of God (Luke 22:69; Acts

2:23; 7:55) and is there making intercession for all His saints (Hebrews 7:25; Romans 8:34). Jesus is praying for us. He never forgets us. He is always interceding on our behalf directly to God the Father at His throne in heaven.

One of the prayers Jesus uttered on earth, still flowing across His lips in heaven today, is – *I am no longer in the world; and yet they themselves are in the world, and I come to Thee. Holy Father, keep them in Thy name, the name which Thou hast given Me, that they may be one, even as We are one…I do not ask Thee to take them out of the world, but to keep them from the evil one…sanctify them in the truth; Thy word is truth* (John 17:11,15,17). The Greek word Jesus used in this prayer and translated *keep* means to watch over and guard, hold in custody, and preserve. Those meanings speak loudly about security. Jesus is the perfect prayer warrior, always praying in the will of His Father, and He is praying God holds us in protective custody and preserves all those who genuinely belong to Him in faith.

The Protection

Why do we spend thousands of dollars annually on car insurance, health insurance, life insurance, and homeowners' insurance? For protection! If the house catches fire, a tornado hits it, we are diagnosed with cancer, or a careless driver totals our car, we want the protection insurance provides to cover the expenses associated with those losses. One catastrophic event could bankrupt us into a total loss without such protection.

Without the security of your salvation, one sin, fault or failure would plummet you into *outer darkness; in that place where there shall be weeping and gnashing of teeth* (Matthew 8:12). But Jesus has issued an insurance policy for each one who has genuinely & sincerely committed their lives to Him in faith – *In Him, you also, after listening to the message of truth, the gospel of your salvation; having also believed (PISTEWO), you were sealed in Him with the Holy Spirit of promise* (Ephesians 1:13). The Greek word translated *sealed* is awesome! It refers to a mark or stamp of ownership, such as what a brand serves to a rancher (it marks his livestock as his ownership).

When sending an official scroll document such as a contract in the ancient days, it was customary to seal the document with candle wax. The person authenticating the document would dribble the wax over the opened edge of the scroll to seal it shut, turning his signet ring over into the hot wax to place his personal seal of authority. This assured the recipient of who it came from, and it arrived unopened for no one's eyes but his.

The Holy Spirit is the official seal that marks and authenticates the genuine believer as the ownership of Jesus Christ, securing him until he reaches his destination (heaven) – *the Holy Spirit of God, by whom you were sealed for the day of redemption* (Ephesians 4:30). The indwelling presence of the Holy Spirit (John 14:17) serves as God's brandmark on every true believer in Christ, securing their ownership as His own until their redemption.

The Pledge

The Holy Spirit is not only given as a seal but – *who is given as a pledge of our inheritance, with a view to the redemption of God's own possession* (Ephesians 1:14). Our salvation is secured under an official seal and by a *pledge.* This Greek word refers to an investment given in earnest as a down payment.

When Carol and I were looking at the possibility of building a house early in our marriage, we first encountered the idea of putting up a sum of earnest money. We would pay a certain amount of money which would serve as our earnest commitment to have the contractor build the house contingent upon whether a mortgage company would extend a loan to us. If they did, the money would be applied to the construction cost. If we did not get the loan, we lost the money because it was stipulated in earnest as non-refundable.

See this beautiful analogy carried over into your relationship with God through Christ. Upon your commitment to surrender your heart & life to Jesus Christ as your Savior & Lord, the Holy Spirit entered your life, sealing you as the marked ownership of God. He was God's non-refundable down payment on your life to permanently secure you exclusively as His until the day you are redeemed into His presence in heaven. The Holy Spirit is non-refundable. God does not take Him back based upon His earnest promise. That is an amazing and awesome expression of love and grace. You might like to pause about now and have a little glory shout!

So, considering this discussion, how can a person who claims to believe in Jesus Christ ever reach the point he is willing to denounce that belief, abandon his association with Christ, and fall away from the faith? The explanation most effectively defended from Scripture is that such a person held a mere belief about Christ but never made a genuine commitment of his life to Christ; therefore, his lifestyle ultimately revealed that deficit. I personally don't believe that any true believer in Christ could ever defect from the faith.

It is a sobering reality such dichotomy can exist in the religious community. Still, Jesus declared it so - *"Not everyone who says to Me, 'Lord, Lord,' will enter the kingdom of heaven, but he who does the will of My Father who is in heaven will enter. Many will say to Me on that day, 'Lord, Lord, did we not prophesy in Your name, and in Your name cast out demons, and in Your name perform many miracles?' And then I will declare to them, 'I never knew you; depart from Me, you who practice lawlessness.'"* (Matthew 7:21-23). There is a false assumption in our culture suggesting when persons die, they automatically "gain their angel wings" and go straight to heaven, regardless of what their lifestyle characterized. This assumption is not valid and certainly not Biblical. Jesus declared *unless one is born again, he cannot see the kingdom of God* (John 3:3). Regardless of how difficult it is to justify in our minds, some religious people have never moved their spiritual experience to the necessary next level. They have never really committed their lives to Christ based on what they have come to understand and believe about Him. Therefore, their lives have failed to manifest a lifestyle characteristic of a genuine commitment.

If *falling away from the faith* is not a reference to the possibility of losing one's salvation, it must refer then to some other form of separation. I believe it is possible *doctrines of demons* and *deceitful spirits* are diabolical entities being used under the sovereign control of God (all things are) to serve the plan & purpose of God in separating the true from the false, the genuine from the superficial, and the real from the fake. He allows this process not to create those differences but to reveal how and among whom they already exist.

45

Separation is not a concept foreign to Scripture. Some of the sons of Levi organized an evil revolt against Moses and Aaron in the wilderness. Confronting this opposition, Moses prayed, and God instructed him, saying, *"Separate yourselves from among this congregation, that I may consume them instantly."* (Numbers 16:20). To assure His judgment against the resistance would not affect innocent Israelites, God further instructed, *"Speak to the congregation, saying, 'Get back from around the dwellings of Korah, Dathan and Abiram.'"* (16:24). The Hebrew terms translated *separate* and *get back* both have to do with establishing distance away and apart from. The account reveals how God then brought judgment – *the earth opened its mouth and swallowed them up, their households, and all the men who belonged to Korah, with their possessions. So, they and all that belonged to them went down alive to Sheol; and the earth closed over them, and they perished from the midst of the assembly* (Numbers 16:32-33). The separation was revealed so God's judgment could be justly applied.

Paul said, *Do not be bound together with unbelievers; for what partnership have righteousness and lawlessness, or what fellowship has light with darkness? Or what harmony has Christ with Belial, or what has a believer in common with an unbeliever? Or what agreement has the temple of God with idols?...therefore, come out from their midst and be separate, says the Lord* (II Corinthians 6:14-17). The Greek word for *separate* means to mark off from others by boundaries. We have traditionally used this principle to warn our Christian youth not to enter courtship or marriage relationships with unbelievers or for people not to enter business partnerships with unbelievers. The different values & convictions inherent in these unholy alliances eventually pose issues and problems which often destroy the relationship.

Certainly, we are not saying Christians should have no friendly relations with non-Christians. We work with nonbelievers, go to school with them, live in the same neighborhood, and even have family relationships with them. While we are commissioned to be *the salt of the earth* (Matthew 5:13) and *a light to those in darkness* (Romans 2:19), we must be careful to maintain a distinguishing posture in comparison. It goes back to the third element of PISTEWO (faith), which is a lifestyle. We have committed our lives based on what we believe about God, and our lifestyle demonstrates that commitment, which stands in stark contrast with lost, worldly persons.

John urged believers, *Do not love the world nor the things in the world...for all that is in the world...is not from the Father, but is from the world* (I John 2:15-16). Paul urged believers, *do not be conformed to this world* (Romans 12:2). The Greek word translated *conformed* means fashioned alike or in the same pattern. You can make a cookie look like a star with a cookie-cutter, but it is not a star; it is still a cookie. Genuine believers in Christ are different, and while we may mix and mingle with non-believers, we do not mirror their lifestyle choices and behaviors lest we take on the manner and appearance of the world. We are set apart as holy & righteous unto God. We must always maintain this distinction in our behavioral choices.

Gold is a valuable commodity. The rock or mineral ore that houses gold is worthless and disposable. To separate the gold from the rock, cyanide is often applied. Cyanide is a rapidly acting deadly chemical that kills the body's cells by preventing them from using oxygen. During World War II, the British and American militaries reportedly distributed cyanide pills to pilots and spies working missions behind enemy lines for use if captured by the Nazis or Soviets. This is said to be no longer a practice of our U.S. government. I cite this example because cyanide is a dangerous, deadly chemical. Yet, when applied to rock or mineral ore containing gold, the chemical dissolves the gold from the stone to be collected and processed for its valuable qualities.

Like deadly cyanide separates gold from rock, *deceitful spirits* and *doctrines of demons* serve in part to separate evil from good, fake from genuine, and deceit from truth. Such a separation is taught in Scripture from Jesus Himself – *All the nations will be gathered before Him; and He will separate them from one another, as the shepherd separates the sheep from the goats; and He will put the sheep to His right, and the goats on the left* (Matthew 25:32-33). This speaks of future judgments serving as a separation of the saved from the lost during the last days' events. With our understanding of the dispensational process unfolding in prophetic events, this separation process may be happening even now, empowered through the use of *deceitful spirits* and *doctrines of demons*, ultimately to be completed in those final judgments of the end times.

So, *falling away from the faith* appears to be the personal choice of various individuals which reveals their true spiritual nature, different from what they have presented throughout their lives. In announcing this kind of defection, Joshua Harris, a million-selling author and former pastor of Covenant Life Church in Maryland, refers to his apostasy as a "divorce." He explains he had "undergone a massive shift regarding faith in Jesus. The popular phrase for this is 'deconstruction,' and the Biblical phrase is 'falling away.' By all the measurements that I have for defining a Christian, I am not a Christian."[8]

Former Hillsong worship leader Marty Sampson defected from the Christian faith in 2019. In his Instagram explanation, he said, "Christians can be the most judgmental people on the planet. They can also be some of the most beautiful and loving people, but it is not for me."[9]

Ryan Bell, the former pastor of the Hollywood Adventist Church in California, launched an experiment to live without God at the beginning of 2013 after preaching for 20 years. A year later, he concluded God did not exist. Five years into that decision, he admitted he missed Christianity for a while but not anymore.[10]

Dave Gass, the former pastor of Grace Family Fellowship in Pleasant Hill, Missouri, renounced his Christian faith as a system rife with abuse that caused his "mental and emotional breaks." He said, "After 40 years of being a devout follower, 20 of those being an evangelical pastor, I am walking away from the faith. Even though this has been a massive bomb drop in my life, it has been decades in the making."[11]

---

[8] Paul Edwards, Josh Harris: *"By all the measures that I have for defining a Christian, I am not a Christian,"* July 27, 2019, The Center for the Study of God & Culture, www.godandculture.com.

[9] Relevant, *Hillsong Songwriter Marty Sampson Says He's Losing His Christian Faith,* August 12, 2019, www.relevantmagazine.com.

[10] Leonardo Blair, *Former pastor Ryan Bell on why he abandoned his Christian faith: I gave it my best shot,* October 27, 2019, www.christianpost.com.

[11] Leonardo Blair, *After 40 years, 'megachurch' pastor slams Christianity and quits, deacon claims he had affair,* May 8, 2019, www.christianexaminer.com.

You may be thinking, how can persons like these make such an abrupt choice especially being pastors and preachers? Jesus announced this clear possibility when He said, *"I never knew you; depart from Me, you who practice lawlessness."* (Matthew 7:23). These acted like they were in the faith, but they were not. Their choice to *fall away* was merely a concession of their true quasi-spiritual condition. The Apostle John revealed a simple and basic point of spiritual logic when he concluded, *They went out from us, but they were not really of us; for if they had been of us, they would have remained with us; but they went out, so that it would be shown that they all are not of us* (1 John 2:19). This phenomenon is a separation process facilitated in part through the agents and sinister plans of darkness.

I want to point out one more aspect of this ongoing separation process. There has been a term emerging out of the political climate of the past few years, especially with the radical changes in the Washington administration following the 2020 Presidential election. It is the term "progressive." For years we have defined opposite political and socio-economic sides as "liberal" and "conservative," or "left" and "right." Those considered to be "left-wing liberals" don't like the stigma associated with that label, so a less threatening and more positive designation is served by calling themselves "progressives."

According to Wikipedia, "Progressivism is a political philosophy in support of social reform. In the 21st century, a movement that identifies as progressive is 'a social or political movement that aims to represent the interests of ordinary people through political change and the support of government actions.'"[12]

---

[12] *Progressivism,* Wikipedia: The Free Encyclopedia, en.wikipedia.org.

Modern, familiar names self-associated with this category of politicians include Alexandria Ocasio-Cortez, Ilhan Omar, Rashida Tlaib, Bernie Sanders, Elizabeth Warren, Stacey Abrams, Cory Booker, Pete Buttigieg, and right up to President Joe Biden and Vice President Kamala Harris in the White House. It is interesting that all of these individuals affiliate with the same political party.

As we glean the political landscape of modern American progressivism, what "interests of ordinary people" define the kind of "social reform" which necessitates "political change" and "government action?" We do not have to look far to see that ideology. The current administration has already executed much of its social reform by ordering further advancements in the LGBT agenda, expanding abortion rights, relaxing laws governing illegal immigration, voter registration, & foreign policy while also imposing strict regulations on energy renewal and climate change. These actions carry multi-trillion-dollar price tags that the government will likely use to justify massive tax increases to offset super inflation throughout the American economy.

The difference & distinction is glaringly evident! "Right-wing conservatives" favor more traditional views seeded in the Judeo-Christian values upon which our nation was founded. We oppose reforms and executive actions which legitimize & legalize evil, perversion, and corruption, and establish good as evil and evil as good (Isaiah 5:20). For any student of the Bible who understands prophetic teaching in Scripture, this modern shift in values & ideals is not just political, it is diabolical. It is indicative of the dispensational progress of eschatological revelations moving our nation toward a "new world order" more in line with the coming regime of the Tribulation Antichrist (more on that in volume three).

For now, I just wanted to identify the "progressive" nature of our political environment as fundamentally associated with the *falling-away* separation currently unfolding in our nation and world.

I think this expanded explanation has been necessary for us to gain a clear understanding of what the Scripture teaches so we can properly place in context what the Holy Spirit is saying through Paul about *falling away*.

Let's move on to the next section of our foundational verse.

SURROGATES – Paying Attention to Deceitful Spirits:

Like the examples of those we cited in the previous section, how can a person experience a "divorce" or a "massive shift" in their belief system about Jesus Christ and abruptly conclude Christianity "is not for me?" Paul answers that question. He indicates the decision comes by *paying attention to* an alternate belief system. The Greek word means to turn one's mind toward, give heed, adhere to, or become addicted to, even to the point of guarding & protecting the tenants of the alternate belief system. These terms define a clear & abrupt about-face accompanied by an aggressive and stubborn defense of the new order.

How is this alternate belief system promoted and perpetuated? Paul again provides the answer. Such persons have been *paying attention to* the alternate ideologies espoused by *deceitful spirits*. They are the surrogates or carriers of these tenants of darkness & evil. The Greek word refers to evil spirits who make up – *the rulers, powers, the world forces of darkness, and the spiritual forces of wickedness in the heavenly places* (Ephesians 6:12). There is a supernatural world of darkness that serves as the domain of Satan and all his principalities, personalities, and powers of evil. Like Satan himself, they – *prowl about like a roaring lion, seeking someone to devour* (I Peter 5:8), and many fall victim to their assault!

How is that possible? Individuals like Joshua Harris, Dave Gass, Ryan Bell, and Marty Sampson can be characterized as having been *once enlightened and have tasted of the heavenly gift and have been made partakers of the Holy Spirit, and have tasted the good word of God and the powers of the age to come, and then have fallen away* (Hebrews 6:4-6). This passage refers to enlightened individuals who have a good head knowledge of spiritual things but never gain a genuine heart knowledge because they never really commit their lives to Christ based on what they have come to understand & believe about Him. How can they turn away from such godly truths? There is a simple answer; because they choose to listen attentively to, believe in, and commit their life to a lie.

Being evil spirits, these surrogates are *deceitful* spirits. The Greek word is PLANOS, where we get our English word, planet, and it has an interesting etiology. The word described a planet's orbit around the central source in its galaxy. It gradually evolved to be a word used to describe a wandering vagabond using deception & corruption to obtain his alms. Eventually, the term was applied to anyone who wandered away into any erroneous or false doctrine. The word describes the surrogate and the message or spirit inherent in the surrogate. Accordingly, anyone who embodies the message of a *deceitful spirit* can be labeled a deceptive spirit, false teacher, false prophet, or antichrist because he embodies the *spirit of antichrist* (I John 4:3).

We must never forget how Jesus characterized Satan and his network of evil – *the devil... does not stand in the truth because there is no truth in him. Whenever he speaks a lie, he speaks from his own nature, for he is a liar and the father of lies* (John 8:44). If Satan is speaking, Satan is lying! It stands only to reason that the devil's nature will also be the nature of his demonic spirits, and the deception that marks his evil nature will also mark theirs.

Deceit involves disguise, and the mask must look genuine, authentic, and right to be effective for recruiting – *And no wonder, for even Satan disguises himself as an angel of light* (II Corinthians 11:14). It is easy to buy into something when it looks right, sounds right, feels right, and makes some sense to one's rationale. We will develop this further in volume two, but know it is a highly effective method for the apostasy we are seeing and will continue to see as the end draws near. It is facilitating the separation process currently underway.

STANDARD – Doctrines of Demons:

The Greek word translated *doctrines* is the word DIDASKOLOS, which refers to a specific teaching, set of instructions, defined precepts, values, and convictions, all of which become a belief system of doctrine. The *doctrines* of which Paul speaks originates with Satan and his demons, again referring to the evil *spirits* of the domain of darkness – *a wisdom which does not come down from above, but is earthly, natural, and demonic* (James 3:15).

As true believers in Christ, we hold to a standard of Biblical principles, precepts, and defined spiritual truths which guide and enrich our lives. They are based on the holiness and righteousness of God. There is another standard in dark contrast to the standard of God's Word. It is the standard of evil, wickedness, and all which opposes God embodied in the person & purpose of Satan and his army of demonic spirit beings.

They are loose in this world, working *to deceive the whole world* (Revelation 12:9)...*having great wrath, knowing that (they have) only a short time* (Revelation 12:12). The future fate of Satan has been set since eternity past – *And the devil who deceived them was thrown into the lake of fire and brimstone, where the beast and the false prophet are also; and they will be tormented day and night forever and ever* (Revelation 20:10). This sentence has not changed and will be carried out according to the declared verdict of God. All the sinister forces of evil know this and know there is very little time left for them to do whatever bidding they can. So, driven by hatred & rage toward God, they work feverishly to wreak all the havoc possible on everything having to do with God while they still have time.

That brings us to the purpose of this trilogy of volumes. What defines this opposing standard? What kind of belief system is so persuasive it is highly successful in causing the apostasy of many, separating the genuine from the superficial, the real from the fake, and the truth from a lie? More specifically, what constitutes doctrines of demons? Can such a belief system be defined in a similar way other belief systems are defined? As I thought about those questions and what appears to be noticeably operating in these later times, several prominent doctrines came to light:

- Doctrine of Deity & Dominion
- Doctrine of Deception

- Doctrine of Deviation
- Doctrine of Division
- Doctrine of Death

We will explore each of these doctrines in great detail in Volume 2 and expand on the applications for how they are being employed in various ways with people, leadership, political agendas, legislative & judicial decisions, behaviors, and lifestyle choices throughout our nation & world. We will also define how their influence leads the world into a blind acceptance of the most sinister lie of all - the coming Antichrist leader of the Tribulation Period is the real Christ.

In Volume 3, our focus will be on deliverance. How can we escape the horrific judgments of the Tribulation Period when evil runs rampant? If we find ourselves oppressed by demonic strongholds, how can we break free of these diabolical powers assaulting our lives? What is spiritual warfare, and how do we withstand this raging battle with the forces of darkness? John reminds believers we have a power within us *greater* than any in Satan's realm (I John 4:4). He and his principalities can be conquered, and their attacks on anyone's life can be subdued and defeated. We define those measures for victory in Volume 3.

However, we must expose the diabolical network of darkness through which these doctrines operate in this first volume. There is a *system established* in this network, specific *strategies enacted*, and various *schemes employed* to affect its ultimate objectives.

THE DIABOLICAL NETWORK OF EVIL: THE SYSTEM ESTABLISHED

O ur youngest son has been very successful at competitive golf since he was eight years old. His first big victory came when he topped the leader board in the 10-year-old boy's division during the Arkansas qualifier for the 2005 U.S. Kids Golf World Championship. Our family packed up our Toyota 4Runner and headed northeast. Austin joined some 2,000 junior golfers from around the nation & the world for the championship tournament played at Ford's Colony Country Club in Williamsburg, Virginia.

The tournament schedule allowed for a free day between Austin's practice round on the course and the tournament's opening round. We took advantage of that day and drove the short distance to our nation's capital in Washington, D.C. The first "National Treasure" box office hit movie had just been released and the line to tour the famous National Archive was backed up a block down Constitution Avenue. Once inside, we couldn't help but imagine standing next to "Ben Gates" and "Riley Poole" as we viewed the original documents of the United States Constitution and the Bill of Rights.

A particular clause in the Bill of Rights states, "Congress shall make no law respecting an establishment of religion." This provision not only forbids the government from establishing an official religion but also prohibits government actions unduly favoring one religion over another. However, some government action implicating religion is permissible and even unavoidable."[13]

The clause served our nation well for over 150 years. Then as diversity increased across our culture, challenges to specific laws & practices related to the "Establishment Clause" became more frequent. Vashti McCollum eventually brought a case before the Supreme Court in 1947, objecting to religious education classes in an Illinois public school.[14] Since then, numerous decisions have been handed down to meet challenges related to religious monuments erected on state & federal grounds and buildings, prayers in public schools and sports events, the teaching of Biblical creationism in science classes, holding any religious meetings on school campuses, etc. These challenges & decisions have managed many to coin the famous phrase, "Separation of Church & State," which appears nowhere in the Constitution or Bill of Rights.

The first public official to use any semblance of that phrase was Roger Williams, founder of Rhode Island. He argued that an authentic Christian church would be possible only if there were a "wall or hedge of separation" between the "wilderness of the world"

---

[13] Legal Information Institute: Open Access to Law Since 1992, *Establishment Clause,* Cornell Law School, law.cornell.edu.

[14] James Van Patten, *McCollum v. Board of Education,* March 8, 1948, Britannica, www.britannica.com.

and "the garden of the church." He believed any government involvement in the church would corrupt the church.[15]

The most famous use of the phrase was by Thomas Jefferson in his 1802 letter to the Danbury Baptist Association of Connecticut. In the letter, Jefferson declared when the American people adopted the Establishment Clause, they built a "wall of separation between the church and state." In Jefferson's colony of Virginia, the Anglican Church had long been the state-established church. He and fellow Virginian, James Madison, believed state support for a particular religion or any religion was improper because it would compel citizens to support through taxation a faith they did not follow, thereby violating their rights to religious liberty.[16]

So, the intent was for the government not to form a government-established church and thereby tax its citizens to support that church through compliance, a clear violation of religious freedom. Jefferson's and Madison's use of the word "separation" has evolved over the centuries to mean what it was never intended to mean; that is, the church has no right to influence the government or the laws of the land in any way whatsoever. The government does what it wants, the church does what it wants, and the two never mix or mingle, especially regarding laws and policies.

If you stop to think about that concept, you might see how ludicrous it really is. Common laws of the land prosecute & penalize

---

[15] John M. Barry, *God, Government, and Roger Williams' Big Idea: The Puritan minister originated a principle that remains contentious to this day-separation of church and state,* January 2012, www.smithsonianmag.com.

[16] Hana M. Ryman and J. Mark Alcorn, *The First Amendment Encyclopedia Presented by the John Seigenthaler Chair of Excellence in First Amendment Studies,* 2009, mtsu.edu.

citizens for such things as murder, theft, and rape. Is it mere coincidence the Bible declares murder, theft, and rape to be sin and issues commands & penalties against those violations? Many aspects of the ancient Jewish Judicial Law still influence the laws which govern our nation today. Yet, any display of the Ten Commandments in a state or federal courthouse is declared in violation of the "Separation of Church & State." Am I the only one who sees the glaring inconsistency in that?

The "Separation of Church & State" has become a whipping stick on the part of many to beat down any effort of the religious community to preserve the ideals and integrity of the Judeo-Christian values upon which our nation was founded. If we oppose any ethical or moral issue in our culture, we are branded as violators of "the Separation of Church & State" and told to go back to our little church buildings and mind our own business. No consideration is given to the fact even though we are members of the church, we are still citizens of the state and have a right to have our voices heard in both arenas.

Is this a battle between citizens? Is it a battle between legislators, judicial branches, political parties, and constituencies? Paul gives us a keen insight which cannot be overlooked as we maneuver this challenging question – *For our struggle is not against flesh and blood, but against the rulers, against the powers, against the world forces of this darkness, against the spiritual forces of wickedness in the heavenly places* (Ephesians 6:12). If we read Paul's words with spiritual discernment, we understand this modern struggle is something far deeper and more sinister than a difference between Democrats and Republicans; or those in favor of casino gambling and those against it; or those who are pro-life and those who are pro-choice; or those who favor traditional marriage and those who promote same-sex marriage, etc. Those issues are just the "bombs bursting in air."

It is not a fight between this Senator and that Congressman or this Administration and the previous administration. It is not a fight with this city councilman, that county alderman, or this mayor and that governor. It is *NOT against flesh and blood!* What is it, then? It is a conflict deeply embedded in a sinister network of evil operating full force in our nation and world. Paul defines this network environment as being in *heavenly places*. We will explain this place more specifically later, but understand it is not a state or federal capitol building or a courtroom; it is in the invisible realm of the supernatural world which serves as Satan's war room.

Think with me for a moment about time. We think primarily about the *present* time because that is where we exist and experience life with our five basic senses (seeing, hearing, feeling, taste & scent). We also think about the *future* as we plan, prepare, and work out details in the present, which position us in more favorable ways for the future. Our view of the *past* is limited to history and what we have learned from it, whether our personal history or that of the world around us.

Three panoramic periods can be gleaned from the Biblical narrative.

Eternity Present

Eternity present denotes where we are in the here and now of our spiritual journey with God. The Bible, serving as our standard and guide, is always pertinent and relevant to our lives. Even though it is a book of ancient history and thoughts which span some 4,000 years, it is ever-present in its active commands, principles, and precepts. The applicable elements of Biblical truth are just as real today as they were 4,000 years ago. From this standpoint, the content of Scripture is eternally present – *My words shall not pass away* (Matthew 24:35), Jesus declared.

Eternity Future

Eternity Future speaks of prophetic events in Scripture yet to unfold in our future. These would include events identified as the Rapture of the Church followed by the Seven-Year Tribulation Period, the Second Coming of Jesus Christ and the establishment of His One-Thousand Year Millennial Reign, the Battle of Armageddon, the Great White Throne Judgment, the New Heaven & the New Earth with the New Jerusalem. We look to these events with great hope and expectation as we joyfully anticipate our future eternity with God.

We are accustomed to thinking about eternity present and eternity future as students of the Bible. Yet, we are not so prone to think about a third panoramic period presented in Scripture - Eternity Past.

Eternity Past

The inspired words of John reveal to us – *In the beginning, was the Word, and the Word was with God, and the Word was God. He was in the beginning with God* (John 1:1-2). We understand clearly from the text John is referring to Jesus, the second person of the Godhead Trinity, because he specifies – *the Word became flesh and dwelled among us, and we beheld His glory, glory as of the only begotten of the Father, full of grace and truth* (John 1:14).

The inspired words of Moses reveal to us – *In the beginning, God created the heavens and earth. And the earth was formless and void, and darkness was over the surface of the deep, and the Spirit of God was moving over the surface of the waters* (Genesis 1:1-2). So, from these verses of Scripture, we learn when Bible history began, God the Father, God the Son, and God the Holy Spirit were all three present and active in the creation process.

However, that does not mean Genesis 1:1 was the beginning point with God, Jesus, or the Holy Spirit. Jesus made a revealing statement – *Truly, truly, I say to you, before Abraham was born, I am* (John 8:58). When Moses was wrangling with God over being the one sent to free the Hebrews from Egyptian slavery, he wanted to know what to tell them when asked by what authority he was presenting himself – *Thus you shall say to the sons of Israel, "I AM has sent you* (Exodus 3:14). The unique tense of this expression simply dictates that with God, Jesus, and the Holy Spirit, all three presently are (eternity present), always will be (eternity future), and always have been (eternity past). There has never been a starting point or an ending point with the God-head Trinity. They always are.

With that in mind, let us turn to a revealing eye-witness report from Jesus – *I was watching Satan fall from heaven like lightning* (Luke 10:18). First, we must establish the context. Always interpret & apply a passage of Scripture within its context. Too many words and phrases of Scripture are taken out of context and thereby wrongly interpreted and erroneously applied. I always want to be careful not to do that.

In Luke 10, Jesus sent out seventy-two of his followers to do the work of spreading the Gospel and ministering to people. They experienced a successful and gratifying evangelistic campaign. When they returned, they joyfully gave Jesus their missions report which included – *even the demons are subject to us in Your name* (Luke 10:17). Jesus affirmed *I was watching*. In other words, "Yes, guys. I know. I saw it. Those demons were coming out of those people fast as lightning!" He was rejoicing with them.

Note particularly the grammar of the Greek tense refers to a continuous action. The imperative tense used here denotes an event that happens at some point in the past, the effects of which are still active in the present and continue to be in the future. In the context, those demons were cast out, they are still cast out, and they will remain cast out of those persons who were delivered from them. It was not just the demons Jesus was watching, but as the text indicates, namely Satan.

This would suggest two things:

First, a **principality perspective.** Jesus saw Satan and the demons those disciples exorcized as part of one diabolical network or principality of corporate evil. The victory they experienced over those demons was a victory over Satan himself. Casting out demons is essentially the same as casting out Satan, who provides the sinister power behind them. As we are one with Christ, demonic spirits are one with Satan.

Secondly, I see a **panoramic perspective.** When we combine the observation of Jesus as continuous action effected in past time, along with the omniscient (all-knowing) and omnipresent (ever-present) qualities of His divine nature, we are not violating the context to suggest Jesus was able to span the panoramic landscape of eternity past, eternity present and eternity future and witness the fall of Satan. Jesus saw Satan fall in the past, He saw Satan's demons cast out in this Gospel account, and He sees into the future when the devil and all his demons & followers will be cast into the Lake of Fire in the end. All of this is Biblically true.

If the fall of Satan from heaven was a past event, when could it have taken place? We turn to several Biblical prophets to get an answer presented from three related perspectives.

Beauty

In Ezekiel 28, two men are identified. One is the *leader of Tyre* (28:1), and the other is the *king of Tyre* (28:12). From specific things revealed about each one in the text, it appears the *leader of Tyre* is a historical official while the *king* is not. Tyre was an ancient country during the time of Ezekiel's prophecy and, like all other countries of the ancient world, likely had a king, prince, or ruler of some kind over it.

There are specific descriptions in the text assigned explicitly to the *king of Tyre,* however, which could not possibly be ascribed to a human man. Therefore, it is the conclusion of many Bible students God is using the evil characteristics of the *king* to characterize the diabolical nature influencing the *leader*, and in doing so, to personify Satan's character & experience in eternity past. Note with me three.

First, he was an **angelic being** - *You were created... the anointed cherub who covers* (28:14,16). You will recall the cherubim covered the Ark of the Covenant to protect it. This also denoted a position closest to the presence of God, which the Ark represented to God's people. So, *the anointed cherub* speaks to the highest position of superiority over all the other angelic beings of heaven. No earthly king could ever hold such a supernatural origin.

Secondly, he was an **angelic beauty** - *You had the seal of perfection, full of wisdom and perfect in beauty* (28:12)...*you were blameless in your ways from the day you were created* (28:15). Like all which God created in heaven, Satan (sometimes named Lucifer), in his original form, was perfect, blameless, and beautiful. He held these three qualities highest and among those he was most proud of, which ultimately became his undoing. No such perfect qualities could ever describe an earthly king.

Thirdly, he was an **angelic braggart** - *Unrighteousness was found in you. By the abundance of your trade you were internally filled with violence and you sinned* (28:15-16)...*your heart was lifted up because of your beauty; you corrupted your wisdom by reason of your splendor* (28:17)...*by the multitudes of your iniquities in the unrighteousness of your trade, you profaned your sanctuaries* (28:18). Most like this earthly leader of Tyre, and the reason Satan is personified through him, pride took over, and sinful rebellion reigned.

The prophet Ezekiel provides a perspective of beauty regarding Satan in eternity past. Let's move to a New Testament prophet and gain the second perspective.

Battle

In his Revelation vision, the apostle John describes two battles resulting in Satan's expulsion from heaven. The first reference is – *a great red dragon* (in the book of Revelation, the *dragon* always represents Satan)…*swept away a third of the stars of heaven and threw them to the earth* (Revelation 12:4). This battle happened at some point near the time of Christ's birth in Bethlehem since reference is made to a *woman* (12:1) representing Israel, giving birth to a *child* (12:2,5), who represents Jesus. For sure, it occurred before the death, burial, resurrection, and ascension of Christ because John reveals *her child was caught up to God and to His throne* (12:5), most likely a reference to the ascension of Jesus in Acts 1:9-11.

The second battle is described a few verses later – *And there was war in heaven, Michael and his angels waging war with the dragon. The dragon and his angels waged war, and they were not strong enough, and there was no longer a place found for them in heaven. And the great dragon was thrown down, the serpent of old who is called the devil and Satan, who deceives the whole world; he was thrown down to the earth, and his angels were thrown down with him* (Revelation 12:7-9). Scholars believe this battle occurs during the first half of the Tribulation period because of the reference to 1,260 days in which Israel is nourished by God (12:6). This amount of time constitutes one-half (3.5 years) of the seven-year Tribulation period as calculated by the ancient Jewish calendar consisting of a 360-day year.

Many don't realize that Satan has had access to God's presence in heaven throughout eternity past, present, and somewhat into the future. His primary effort on all these occasions has been to *accuse* believers (Revelation 12:10). Two familiar instances stand out in Scripture:

One has to do with Job – *Now there was a day when the sons of God came to present themselves before the Lord, and Satan also came among them. The Lord said to Satan, "From where do you come?" Then Satan answered the Lord and said, "From roaming about on the earth and walking around on it." The Lord said to Satan, "Have you considered My servant Job? For there is no one like him on the earth, a blameless and upright man, fearing God and turning away from evil." Then Satan answered the Lord, "Does Job fear God for nothing? Have You not made a hedge about him and his house and all that he has, on every side? You have blessed the work of his hands, and his possessions have increased in the land. But put forth Your hand now and touch all that he has; he will surely curse You to Your face." Then the Lord said to Satan, "Behold, all that he has is in your power, only do not put forth your hand on him." So Satan departed from the presence of the Lord* (Job 1:6-12). Satan appeared before God a second time for permission to attack Job further (2:1-6). As we know from the story, Satan took the lives of all Job's children and destroyed his properties before finally attacking his body with open sores and horrible sickness. God proved Job to be faithful & true, healed Job, restored his fortunes, and added to his family (42:10-17).

In another instance and just before Jesus was arrested, tried, and crucified, Satan gained an audience before God in Heaven about Peter. Jesus announced to Peter the substance of that conversation –

Simon, Simon, behold, Satan has demanded permission to sift you like wheat; but I have prayed for you, that your faith may not fail; and you, when once you have turned again, strengthen your brothers (Luke 22:31-32). When things started to go down regarding Jesus, Peter bailed and denied even knowing Him; not just once, but three times. In shame, Peter ran off into hiding. Following His resurrection, Jesus forgave Peter and welcomed him back into fellowship. As a result, Peter became one of the founding apostles and great leaders of the early New Testament church. The prayer of Jesus won the victory in Peter's life.

That brings back a thought we posed earlier about people saying they will pray for you, and you wonder if they ever remember to do so; regardless of whether they do or don't, Jesus always does! He is at the right hand of God in heaven always making intercession for you and me (Hebrews 7:25). He always prays in the exact will of the Father with just the right words when we cannot find the words with which to pray, or even begin to know what God's will is (Romans 8:26-27). When we are under attack by Satan and his demonic spirits, Jesus is always powerfully praying for our victory, just as He did for Peter!

Bolt

The second battle John records in Revelation 12:7-9 denotes the last time Satan and any of his *angels* (demon spirits) will ever have access again to God in heaven – *(they) were not strong enough, and there was no longer a place found for them in heaven. And the great dragon was thrown down...to the earth, and his angels were thrown down with him* (Revelation 12:8-9). Even though this is the final battle Satan will wage in heaven, it was not the first as John shows us. We can assume such confrontations may have been staged many times over the eternal panoramic periods of time even though Scripture only reveals several of them.

Two Old Testament prophets report such an expulsion – *I have cast you as profane from the mountain of God, and I have destroyed you, O covering cherub…I cast you to the ground…I have turned you to the ashes on the earth* (Ezekiel 28:16-18). As with the king of Tyre, God uses the evil ruler Nebuchadnezzar to personify Satan in Isaiah's prophecy – *How you have fallen from heaven, O star of the morning, son of the dawn! You have been cut down to the earth* (Isaiah 14:12-13). Jesus was watching each time these conflicts unfolded, and each time Satan was cast out of God's presence.

As with this second and final battle in Revelation 12, Satan is joined in the campaign by *his angels* (12:7). In the former battle, we learn his expulsion resulted in *a third of the stars of heaven* cast down to the earth with him (12:4). The word *stars* is a Biblical reference most often ascribed to angelic beings God created in eternity past – *Where were you when I laid the foundation of the earth…when the morning stars sang together and all the sons of God shouted for joy?* (Job 38:4,7).

An interesting question to pose is just how many *a third* might be? To get an idea, we note an earlier reference by John when he witnessed – *the voice of many angels around the throne…the number of them was myriads of myriads, and thousands of thousands* (Revelation 5:11). The Greek term *myriads* was an undefined number used to describe more than could be counted (like our "gazillion" – not an actual number, but more than anyone can calculate). *Thousands of thousands* further enumerate this

70

incalculable number! Whatever number this would be (an astronomical number for sure), Satan acquired *one-third* of them as recruits for his network of evil servants. So, it can be assumed the forces of darkness which serve in Satan's diabolical system could number well into the millions upon millions! This is how many demon spirits are at Satan's disposal and how many *deceitful spirits* serve as surrogates to espouse *doctrines of demons* across our world. That is staggering and sobering!

All these demon angels, along with their leader, Satan, have been cast down to the earth where they remain today. We know at least one such expulsion from heaven to earth occurred in eternity past because the first place we see Satan show up in the pages of Scripture is *in Eden, the garden of God* (Ezekiel 28:13). There, he tempts Eve and Adam to disobey God concerning the forbidden fruit, facilitating his first sustained victory – the fall of man (Genesis 3).

So, the diabolical system of Satan exists in the invisible supernatural realm of the earth. Even though this might be a concept difficult for many people to wrap their minds around, Paul clearly describes God's creation as including – *both in the heavens and on earth, visible and invisible, whether thrones or dominions or rulers or authorities* (Colossians 1:16). The writer of Hebrews further clarified – *By faith, we understand that the worlds were prepared by the word of God so that what is seen was not made out of things which are visible* (Hebrews 11:3). Paul understood and accepted the reality of the supernatural realms – *while we look not at the things which are seen, but at the things which are not seen; for the things that are seen are temporal, but the things which are not seen are eternal* (II Corinthians 4:18).

There is undeniably a supernatural world that exists beyond the ability of our human physical eyes to see. However, Scripture records the accounts of some who have been given the privilege to peer into this portal – Moses, Elijah, John, Paul, Peter, James. It houses both a holy & righteous realm where God and His people reside (Paradise) and a wicked & evil realm where Satan, his followers, and his network of demons abide (Hades). Jesus told us there is *a great chasm fixed* between the two making no access on either side to the other possible, or any occupant from leaving either place (Luke 16:26).

May I take us aside for a moment? There has been a modern fascination with the paranormal and ghost-hunting antics. Groups and organizations visit places reputed to be haunted by departed persons. They set up sophisticated audio & video equipment with hopes of capturing the recording of a ghost. Syndicated television programs showing these adventures rank among the highest in network viewership.

Paul teaches that when believers in Christ are *absent from the body,* (in death) we are immediately *present with the Lord* (II Corinthians 5:6,8). At the same time, lost persons who have died are imprisoned in *Hades*, the holding place of the unrighteous dead until the *Great White Throne* Judgement when they will be eternally sentenced to the *Lake of Fire* (Luke 16:26; Revelation 20:11-15).

With a clear understanding of these two Scriptural insights, we can see how it is impossible for departed human spirits to be lingering in earthly places. That leaves only one other possibility if indeed these ghost hunters are finding paranormal presence and manifestations – they are demonic beings meant to deceive and devour. When you dance with demons, you can expect to eventually be assaulted and afflicted.

Scripture helps us further define these supernatural realms. In describing his ascent into heaven, Paul described himself as being – *caught up to the third heaven* (II Corinthians 12:2). He further specifies the place of the "third heaven" as being *Paradise* (12:4). By simple deduction, if there is a "third heaven," it would stand to reason there is also a "first" and "second" heaven.

In contrasting the lives of the Ephesian believers with their former life before coming to Christ, Paul indicated they – *formerly walked according to the course of this world, according to the prince of the power of the air, of the spirit that is now working in the sons of disobedience* (Ephesians 2:2). The Greek word Paul uses for *air* refers specifically to the atmospheric layer surrounding our planet, enriched with the oxygen we breathe. This would denote the "first" heaven.

That leaves the "second" heaven to likely be the expanse beyond earth's atmosphere – outer space, the universe which holds all the planets, galaxies & stars.

In being cast down to the earth, Satan has been given temporary & limited dominion as the *prince of the power of the air*. This word refers to a ruler, commander, chief, or leader in the Greek text. Jesus referred to Satan as *the ruler* (same Greek word) *of this world* (John 12:31). Paul referred to Satan as *the god of this world* (II Corinthians 4:4), and it is said Satan has *power* over the air (the first & second heavens). This Greek word refers to the ability to exercise control, manage and execute all the functions of the air.

Not only does Satan occupy this domain, but his myriads of demons accompany it with him. Paul clarified to us – *Our struggle is not against flesh and blood, but against the rulers, against the powers, against the world forces of this darkness, against the spiritual forces of wickedness in the heavenly places* (Ephesians 6:12). Here again, the heavenly places are identified as the realm of wickedness & evil where Satan and his demonic forces exist and operate.

This dominion not only involves the air but also includes the earth. Satan was cast down to the earth, and when he met Jesus in the temptation wilderness, he – *took Him to a very high mountain and showed Him all the kingdoms of the world, and their glory; and he said to Him, "All these things will I give You if You will fall down and worship me."* (Matthew 4:8-10). How could Satan offer to Jesus that which was not at least somewhat his to convey? Ultimately, of course – *all things have been created by (Jesus) and for (Jesus)* (Colossians 1:16); so, it all belonged to Jesus regardless, but Satan has been extended temporary and limited rule over the earth and the power of the air.

This is important to remember when devastating earthquakes, volcanoes, viruses, bacteria, pestilence, hurricanes, tornadoes, tsunamis, floods, fires, and such destroy property and take away lives. Satan has all the power and authority to manage & execute the massive destruction of these forces of nature. He can do this because he holds temporary & limited control over the ground and the air where these natural forces emerge.

This may also explain the phenomenon with UFOs (Unidentified Flying Objects) and so-called "extraterrestrial encounters." Now, I know you think I may have just flipped out in science fiction Lah-Lah Land or fallen into the confusing & conflicting world of conspiracy theories, but wait for it. Our government has revealed enough to us as citizens to learn there have been certain occasions when unexplainable sightings & encounters have occurred. In May of 2020, for instance, the New York Times reported between 2013-2019, Navy pilots encountered eight "unidentified aerial vehicles" while flying practice maneuvers. In April of 2020, the Department of Defense at the Pentagon released three unclassified videos in 2004 and 2015 depicting unidentified objects captured and moving at incredible speeds.[17]

The New York Times reports the Pentagon appears to be still collecting information on "anomalous aerial vehicles." In the section titled "Advanced Aerial Threats" in the Intelligence Authorization Act for Fiscal Year 2021, the government mentions for the first time the "Unidentified Aerial Phenomenon Task Force," which resides at the Office of Naval Intelligence. The purpose of this task force, which is not classified but deals with classified matters, is standardizing the collection and reporting on sightings of unexplained aerial vehicles and sharing those findings with the public.[18]

I am reasonably confident there are no actual aliens flying spaceships to Earth from other planets. Still, there may well be demonic beings of Satan's diabolical force manifesting themselves in such ways to distract us, distort our understanding of God's

---

[17] Ralph Blumenthal and Leslie Kean, *Navy Reports Describe Encounters with Unexplained Flying Objects,* updated July 24, 2020, The New York Times, www.nytimes.com.
[18] Julian Barnes, *Pentegon Forms Group to Examine Unexplained Aerial Sightings,* November 25, 2021, www.nytimes.com.

creation, confuse us, build fear in us, and perhaps even harm us in these celestial ways. It is not beyond the power of Satan to do so as he holds certain dominion over the "second" heaven – outer space and the universe.

I realize this idea is really "out there" for most folks to imagine. Still, you must consider a supernatural world has access to supernatural powers, which serve both the holy realms of God and the evil empires of Satan. John revealed that *spirits of demons will perform signs* (Revelation 16:14) during the Tribulation Period. *Signs* is a Greek word referring to an unusual occurrence that transcends the ordinary course of nature (miracles and wonders).

The false prophet who will be the religious leader and right-hand man to the antichrist during the Tribulation Period is said by John to be supernaturally empowered to – *perform great signs so that he even makes fire come down out of heaven to the earth in the presence of men. And he deceives those who dwell on the earth because of the signs which it was given him to perform* (Revelation 13:13-14). Jesus revealed to us *there will be signs in the sun and moon and stars and on the earth dismay among nations, in perplexity at the roaring of the sea and the waves* (Luke 21:25). So, the Bible affirms there exists within the evil realm of Satan's diabolical system, supernatural powers to do unusual and miraculous things in the air and on the ground to deceive and destroy people and lands.

Make no mistake about it. These powers exist even now, and it stands to reason the forces of darkness are employing them to deceive. So, don't dispel anything as mere conspiracy, fantasy, or make-believe just because it seems unbelievable or impossible. This potential is real! It is real because Satan is real, and his massive diabolical system is real.

The church has allowed the world to bully & beat us into our quiet corner with the "Separation of Church & State" clobbering stick far too long! Where that might have had its times of appropriateness throughout past decades, things have changed! 2020 served as a major shifting point in our nation and world. It provided the forces of evil a diabolical opportunity for what is being internationally coined as "The Great Reset" (more on that in Volume 3). The kind of radical evil being legitimized and legalized across our nation and the world demands the church to "get on the battlefield with our Lord." It is no longer appropriate to be quiet. It is time to revolt against these powers, these world forces of darkness, and these spiritual forces of wickedness in the heavenly places. Unfortunately, our nation's cultural and political arenas serve as one of the hot combat zones where we must *stand firm against the schemes of the devil* (Ephesians 6:11).

We have explored the established system, and before we can grasp the employed schemes, we must next understand the enacted strategies of this diabolical network.

THE DIABOLICAL NETWORK OF
EVIL: THE STRATEGIES ENACTED

Suppose I was to ask you who the most significant military war strategists of the past several centuries would be. You might think of Thomas "Stonewall" Jackson, one of the greatest Confederate Generals of the American Civil War. In that same war era, you might think of great names like Ulysses S. Grant or Robert E. Lee. You might think of later names such as General Dwight D. Eisenhower, who is said to have turned the tide of World War II, or George S. Patton, Jr., deemed "Old Blood & Guts" for his World War II successes against Germany. You might think of General Douglas MacArthur, whose military brilliance covered both world wars and the Korean War.

According to many historians, Napoleon Bonaparte is credited with being the greatest tactician and military genius of his time. His campaigns formed the basics for military education used throughout the Western world, and much of our war strategy today is still influenced by this great Frenchman. One British general was heard to say the presence of Napoleon on the battlefield made the difference of 40,000 men.[19] Napoleon's understanding of mass warfare and his success in raising, organizing, and equipping mass armies revolutionized the conduct of war and marked the origin of modern warfare. Prussian General Carl von Clausewitz referred to Napoleon as the "god of war."[20]

While attending an event at Ridgecrest Baptist Conference Center many years ago, Carol and I toured the beautiful George W. Vanderbilt *Biltmore Estate* in nearby Asheville, North Carolina. There, we saw a walnut gaming table said to have been owned by Napoleon. Inside the unit's drawer is an inscription claiming upon his death, Napoleon's heart was placed in a silver urn and set on the table before the urn was secured in his casket. The Vanderbilt's reportedly acquired the table from a London Dealer.[21] I remember gazing at the table with a particular fascination at such a morbid claim offered in commemoration of his military prowess.

Napoleon is quoted as saying, "There is no man more pusillanimous than I when I am planning a campaign. I purposely exaggerate all the dangers and all the calamities that the circumstances make possible. I am in a thoroughly painful state of agitation."[22] While not implying anything about Napoleon's spiritual condition, that statement could easily summarize the stratagem behind Satan's diabolical network of evil. We know he is highly agitated, *having great wrath* (Revelation 12:12). We know

---

[19] *Wellington and Napoleon,* www.wellingtoncollection.co.uk.

[20] Andreas Herberg Rothe, *A Prussian in the United States,* October 2003, www.clausewitz.com.

[21] Betsy Lammerding and Knight-Ridder, *A Touch of Class,* June 21, 1992, the Chicago Tribune, www.chicagotribune.com.

[22] David G. Chandler, *The Campaigns of Napoleon,* 1966, Macmillan Publishing Company.

he constantly plans attacks on people as he *prowls about like a roaring lion, seeking someone to devour* (I Peter 5:8). We also know he plans for the worst possible outcome in those attacks because he *comes only to kill, steal, and destroy* (John 10:10).

Some would raise objections to the theme of this book because they would insist it gives too much attention to Satan, an evil being who doesn't deserve the glory of that much focus. While I get that and agree wholeheartedly, I also recognize we are in a state of spiritual warfare (Ephesians 6:10-20). When you are at war, it is always best to know your enemy and the various tactics & strategies he is apt to employ against you.

The 6th Century Chinese General Sun Tzu once said, "If you know the enemy and know yourself, you need not fear the result of a hundred battles. If you know yourself but not the enemy, for every victory gained, you will also suffer a defeat. If you know neither the enemy nor yourself, you will succumb in every battle."[23] As with Napoleon, not implying anything about Tzu's spiritual perspectives, notice the three positional conditions He qualified and how they compare to Satan's approach:

Secure (know yourself; know your enemy):

Security comes in part by knowing yourself spiritually. The Apostle John wrote *He who has the Son has the life; he who does not have the Son of God does not have the life. These things I have written to you who believe in the name of the Son of God, in order that you may know that you have eternal life* (I John 5:12-13). The secure believer in Christ does not have to question or doubt his

---

[23] Sun Tzu's Art of War, *Attack By Stratagem,* 1910, www.suntzusaid.com.

spiritual place with God. He can *know* with complete confidence and assurance he has eternal life in Him because of his faith commitment to Christ.

Security also comes in part by remaining in a state of alertness – *Be of sober spirit, be on alert*, Peter warns us concerning *our adversary the devil* (I Peter 5:8). Satan is our *adversary*, our opponent, and archenemy! The Greek words translated *sober,* and *alert* mean to be clear-minded, wide-awake, and circumspective; that is, looking around every corner, cautious, careful of consequences, and watchful of the danger Satan poses to our lives.

Peter further instructs us to *resist him firm in your faith* (5:9). The Greek word *resist* means to set yourself up against Satan. As believers, we already hold an established position against Satan because of our relationship with God in Christ. Accordingly, we are to continue resisting his approach. We do that by remaining *firm* in our *faith*. The Greek word means to be solid, stable, steadfast, and sure in our faith with all the resources of God's power and might. That comes by walking obediently in God's Word, will, and ways. James affirms this same principle – *Submit therefore to God. Resist the devil and he will flee from you. Draw near to God and He will draw near to you* (James 4:7-8). So, resisting Satan is accomplished by submitting and drawing near to the God of our faith. Only then will Satan *flee* from us. That interesting Greek word means to escape imminent danger by dashing for shelter! If you just run away from Satan, more than likely, he will chase you. But if you run to Jesus, Satan will run the other way!

The secure believer is confident in the Biblical reality that *greater is He who is in you than he who is in the world* (I John 4:4).

The God of heaven, who indwells each believer with the Holy Spirit, is far *greater* (the Greek word is MEGAS, where we get our English prefix, "mega") than the god of this world, Satan. We need not fear his threat. When we stand against the devil, he is already the "weakest link...goodbye!"

Shaken (know yourself but not the enemy):

Unfortunately, there are too many believers whose lives are shaken by the attacks of Satan because they tend to be shallow in their faith rather than firm & secure. They struggle with obedience. They flirt with the world's passions and pleasures, and their loyalties are divided. They fail to submit and draw near to God for necessary strength, wisdom, and spiritual discernment because they neglect the essentials of Bible study, worship, and prayer.

Not only that, but they are also blind to what is happening to them. Their infatuation with the ways of the world is blinding their eyes to the subtle entrapment the forces of darkness are leveraging against them. They fail to be sober and on alert; therefore, are easily ambushed and suffer varying degrees of defeat on the battlefield. Many of these aren't even aware they are on a battlefield. They are clueless a war is unfolding around them and how vulnerable they are because of their ignorance of the enemy and the opposition advancing on every side. No wonder their lives are so shaken with shame, struggles, and shackles.

Shattered (know neither your enemy nor yourself):

Paul noted the believers in the church at Ephesus had *formerly walked according to the course of this world, according to the prince of the power of the air, of the spirit that is now working in the sons of disobedience...and were by nature children of wrath* (Ephesians 2:1-3). In other words, before coming to Christ, all persons are in the devil's army. Their lives are shattered in the lost condition of their sin, destined to spend an eternity separated from God in outer darkness where Satan and all his demonic spirits will also reside.

This fate is obscured from their awareness because *the god of this world has blinded the minds of the unbelieving, that they might not see the light of the gospel of the glory of Christ* (II Corinthians 4:4). Accordingly, they *walk in darkness and do not know where they are going because the darkness has blinded their eyes* (I John 2:11).

Satan already has these persons; he just must invoke specific strategies to keep them from hearing and responding to the gospel message of Christ, which can forgive them of their sins and save them from eternal condemnation. Such a strategy is what Jesus exposed in the Parable of Sower – *When anyone hears the word of the kingdom and does not understand it, the evil one comes and snatches away what has been sown in his heart* (Matthew 13:19). Satan accomplishes this through distraction, distortion, deception, and determent.

We see an example of this strategy when Paul and Barnabas shared the gospel with Sergius Paulus, the proconsul among the Jews. Satan had a Jewish false prophet named Bar-Jesus (aka, Elymas, the magician) in the same room *opposing them, seeking to turn the proconsul away from the faith* (Acts 13:6-8). Paul, discerning very clearly what was going on, *fixed his gaze upon him, and said, "You who are full of all deceit and fraud, you son of the devil, you enemy of all righteousness, will you not cease to make crooked the straight ways of the Lord? And now, behold, the hand of the Lord is against you...* " (13:9-11). Paul picked up on what was happening in the realm of darkness around him because he was *filled with the Holy Spirit* (13:9), and he didn't hesitate to engage the enemy on the battlefield.

Our military would have little chance of defeating enemies like Islamic terrorism if they didn't undergo extensive training on this enemy network's ideologies, tactics, and strategies and how they operate in the battle arena. We spend billions of dollars equipping our intelligence networks and branches of our military on understanding, evaluating, and assessing the governments & military complexes of foreign nations. Hence, if they ever become a threat to the security of the United States, we are not illiterate to their capabilities and resources. Knowing the enemy is essential in warfare, especially spiritual warfare!

We have acquainted ourselves with the established system encompassing Satan's diabolical network. Let's better understand the enacted strategies that guide this evil force of darkness. I would propose four basic strategies.

The Rudimentary Strategies

We have already observed how Scripture has used both the leader of Tyre in Ezekiel and King Nebuchadnezzar in Isaiah to personify Satan's evil character and activities in eternity past.

In John 10, Jesus similarly presents Himself as a *figure of speech* (John 10:6), namely, *the good shepherd* (10:14). Accordingly, we are His sheep who hear His voice and follow Him. Being the Shepherd, He guards the door to the sheepfold, and the only way in is through Him – *I am the way, and the truth, and the life; no one comes to the Father, but through Me* (John 14:6). Only the thief and robber seek to get into the fold *some other way* (10:1) because their purpose is not to join the fold but to attack and scatter it very much like a wolf or some other predator would do in snatching its prey.

If Jesus is personifying salvation, who is the only enemy striving incessantly to keep lost people from coming to Jesus, entering the door of salvation, and becoming a part of His fold? The obvious answer is Satan, so Jesus presents Satan in this illustration as the thief and robber – *The thief comes only to steal and kill and destroy; I came that they may have life and have it abundantly* (John 10:10). This verse alone clearly defines the great contrast between the world of God and the world of Satan.

This is the most fundamental strategy of all the strategies in hell and darkness we might attempt to define. Not only is it rudimentary, but Jesus said it is also exclusive – Satan *comes ONLY* to carry out these three basic strategies. They are his one and only ones, his ultimate bottom-line goals – *to steal, kill and destroy*! Every other is like a sub-strategy to one of these. Whatever any different strategy seeks to accomplish, it ultimately results in one of these three rudimentary strategies:

Steal

Steal is the Greek word KLEPTO, where we get our English word "kleptomaniac," which describes a person driven to steal compulsively. It might be motivated out of greed, covetousness, impoverishment, or just the simple desire to inflict the pain and suffering of loss on others. Whatever the motive, thievery is a driving addiction with a "kleptomaniac."

Ezekiel described Satan's beauty, wisdom, perfection, and unique place in God's presence when he staged his unsuccessful mutiny against God in eternity past. Satan likely lost much of those qualities when he was cast down to the earth. The last thing Satan wants for you and me is to enjoy such good things as he has lost, so he works overtime to rob us of the good things God has blessed us with and the joy that comes with them. We had noted how Satan used this basic strategy against Job when he stole from this faithful servant everything with which God had blessed him in attacking Job's faith and obedience to God.

Destroy

Destroy is a word that carries several related meanings, including efforts that cause loss or render people and things useless. God has a will, plan, and purpose for each of our lives, He lovingly compels us to live out. Walking in the very center of God's will, plan and purpose provides our Christian life with the best happiness and greatest fulfillment. This too is the last thing Satan wants us to experience, so he works overtime to find ways that may cause us to fail, suffer loss, miss out, be picked over, or otherwise interfere with our opportunities and circumstances of life to render us void and useless in the things God desires for us.

If it takes ruining our career to accomplish that, Satan will find a way to try and ruin our career. If it takes putting us in a wheelchair to achieve that, he will find a way to try and put us in a wheelchair. If it takes bankrupting our financial portfolio to accomplish that, he will find a way to try and break our accounts. We are merely tipping the iceberg with these examples, but hopefully, you get the point. Satan wants to destroy you and everything good about your life if he can, and you can count on the fact that he will try.

Kill

To *kill* is the most rudimentary of the three. God's first directive to Adam & Eve in the Garden had to do with the forbidden fruit – *You shall not eat from it or touch it, lest you die* (Genesis 3:3). In reaction to Satan's temptation, they did, and the curse which was wrought dictated that humankind would – *return to the ground because from it you were taken; for you are dust, and to dust you shall return* (3:19-20). The writer of Hebrews sums it up relatively simple – *it is appointed for men to die once* (9:27). Paul did as well – *the wages of sin is death* (Romans 6:23).

Satan wants you dead! He will do anything he can to kill you if he can. Nothing would please Satan more than to see you suffer and die in your sin – *for when sin is accomplished, it brings forth death* (James 1:15). If he cannot kill you, he will attempt to lead you down the road to death by tempting you with sinful choices and lifestyles which will accomplish that end (alcohol, drugs, crime). Why? Because first & foremost, he wants every lost person in hell with him for all eternity, and he knows death seals the deal. Death ends all opportunities to respond to the saving Gospel of Christ and solidifies a person's eternal fate. At the same time, he wants to render useless the work believers can accomplish for the cause of Christ, so attempting to take Christians out of the arena through faults & failures helps to put a dent in Kingdom growth and effectiveness.

In stark contrast, where Satan has the goal of death, Jesus has the goal of life – *the thief comes to…kill; I came that they may have life* (John 10:10). God is the author of life. Satan is the author of death. Satan facilitated the ushering in of death. Jesus severed the *sting* and *victory* of *death* with His accomplished work of redemption on the cross (I Corinthians 15:55). The worst thing a person can say to someone who just lost a loved one in death is some expression of the suggestion, "it just must have been God's will." It has never been, nor shall ever be, God's will for anyone to die! Jesus came so we might have life, not death! It is the devil and sin that bring death. Satan came to kill, steal, and destroy.

We will come back to these points in Scripture often as we detail various doctrines of demons in volume two and how they are being applied in the lives of people today. Kill, steal, and destroy - these three objectives define the rudimentary strategies of Satan's diabolical network of evil, but there are more.

The Reformation Strategies

We hear the word "reform" often in the political arena as it is applied to tax reform, welfare (social) reform, immigration reform, healthcare reform, prison reform, etc. It refers to making changes or restructuring things to improve and increase effectiveness. Unfortunately, the kind of changes reform brings is not always best for the greater good and often serves nothing more than to advance a defined partisan agenda and purpose.

That dynamic makes reformation an attractive basic strategy for Satan's network of evil. The adage, "if it's not broke, don't fix it," means absolutely nothing to Satan. If something is working relatively well, he will try to break it. If it is broken, the last thing he wants to do is fix it if leaving it broken better serves his purpose.

Nothing is broken with God's Word, will, and ways. His ways are holy, and His Word is righteous and true. His ways provide the greatest joy and abundance in your life and mine. However, as we have clarified, those divine benefits are the last things Satan would have us enjoy. He has another purpose, and he needs to attempt every effort of reform he can to change things to fit his evil will and ways better.

Satan is engaged in a basic strategy to reform God's truth and commands and has promoted that reform for thousands of years. It was apparent in Isaiah's day when God declared through the prophet – *Woe to those who call evil good, and good evil; who substitute darkness for light, and light for darkness; who substitute bitter for sweet, and sweet for bitter* (Isaiah 5:20). This strategy is meant to reverse all God has declared holy, righteous, and true. Satan has employed this strategy intensely within our modern world and culture's moral, ethical, and political environments. Many things God's Word has declared evil, dark, and bitter; Satan has managed quite successfully to reverse by infiltrating the ranks of human reasoning, behavioral lifestyles, and civil regulatory practices and reforming them into good, light, and sweet.

An example of this strategic effort is seen very clearly in the way our culture has reformed views on the practice of homosexuality. I contend God's Word explicitly condemns homosexuality as an absolute abomination (Leviticus 18:22; Romans 1:24-27). Satan, however, has infiltrated the ranks of the entertainment & movie industry, the national media, the political, legislative & judiciary branches of our government, and even some aspects within the church to twist God's declaration and reform the thinking of people to accept the LGBT lifestyle as not sinful in any form or fashion. Instead, it is now claimed to be a gift of God such persons are born to indulge with unbridled freedom and divine acceptance. Same-sex marriage is now legal across America and other parts of the world. What God declared as evil, culture has now declared good and legally allowed. We will discuss this issue in greater detail in Volume 2 when exploring the Doctrine of Deviation.

Regardless of what Satan attempts in these ways, God's Word promises – *the evil will bow down before the good, and the wicked at the gates of the righteous* (Proverbs 14:19). If Satan knows this (and there's a good chance he does), he must know ultimately he will not win. However, that doesn't hinder him because he knows before God ultimately defeats his efforts, he can still succeed in destroying and killing the lives of millions of naïve persons who buy into his reformative narrative.

In defining eternity past, present, and future, what we said is God and His Word are *the same yesterday, today, and forever* (Hebrews 13:8). Two things remain eternally present, never changing, and constantly relevant in precept and practice - the character of God and the truth of His Word. What God declared as sin 4,000 years ago is still sin today, regardless of how Satan and his diabolical evil network try to spin it in our modern culture.

All who buy into his narrative will eventually discover what God's Word designates as evil, really is evil; what is dark really is dark, and what is bitter is indeed bitter. When that sobering moment of reality finally sets in, the laughter echoing through the caverns of hell will mock the ignorance and naivety of those who fell for it, and darkness will celebrate its destruction and death on the lives of their victims.

The Replication Strategies

If Satan just showed up and stuck his alluring face in yours and said, "Hey, try this; you'll love it," you'd probably run for your life in terror. He is cunningly intelligent enough to know such an approach would have little chance of working, so he disguises himself. In the Garden before Eve, Satan took on the form of a serpent, apparently a reptile she would not normally have resisted (snakes were not always so threatening and terrifying, ladies).

A strategy experiencing a great deal of success in the operation of Satan's network of evil is the covert approach – *Satan disguises himself as an angel of light, therefore it is not surprising if his servants also disguise themselves as servants of righteousness* (II Corinthians 11:14-15). When a hunter goes into the woods, he wears camouflage to replicate his surroundings. When our military advances into enemy territory, it adorns its outward appearance to replicate the environment so soldiers blend into those surroundings less detected. Satan has deployed a highly effective strategy in our world today by presenting himself and all his representatives as good and light on the outside, even though they remain dark and evil underneath all their righteous camouflage. Jesus described them as – *coming to you in sheep's clothing, but inwardly are ravenous wolves* (Matthew 7:15).

There are popular and respected voices in our world today having the ears of great audiences and who use Scripture and spiritual language to assert such things as abortion, non-marital sex, and the LGBT lifestyle are acceptable ideals. Their arguments have a certain ring of rationale, logic, even some remote theological-sounding sensibility, and psychological insight. This is difficult to admit, but it illustrates the effectiveness in the art of disguise, which no other being is more expert at presenting than Satan and his demonic force.

If you want to find justification for sin in our modern culture, you won't have to look far or long. Around any corner is some book, some speaker, website, blog, YouTube channel, social media account, television program, even some preachers and religious leaders in churches who will give you what you seek – *for the time will come when they will not endure sound doctrine; but wanting to have their ears tickled, they will accumulate for themselves teachers in accordance to their own desires; and will turn away their ears from the truth, and will turn aside to myths* (II Timothy 4:3-4). Did you catch the last word? The Greek word *myth* defines a fictitious narrative or falsehood, which is the essence of Satan and darkness (more on that in Volume 2 when we define the Doctrine of Deception).

This is a highly effective strategy because Satan has representatives in many ranks of education, religion, government, the judicial branches, and fields of psychology and medicine disguised and promoting doctrines of deceit to steal, kill and destroy the lives of millions of people. He is replicating godliness to promote savage ungodliness. Where is all this leading? What is the ultimate goal of darkness? Satan has a plan for rising to power and fulfilling his lust for dominion.

The Ratification Strategies

The covert disguise we have been discussing, along with the reversal of good and evil, is all meant to brainwash and condition our world for the ratification of two men who will eventually rise to the forefront of global government, economics, and religion during the eschatological period Scripture calls the Tribulation. The Bible identifies these two men as the Antichrist and the False Prophet.

They will be the ultimate angels of light. They will adorn the most convincing disguises. They will be so effective the world will embrace & accept them as THE Christ and THE prophet of God. It will be easier for the people of the world to do this because they have been and continue to be indoctrinated to do so for centuries. If Satan can convince individuals now that evil is good and good is evil, he will have little challenge in convincing people later the Antichrist is the real Jesus Christ who you are to worship and serve (we will discuss this in greater detail in volume 3).

On May 27, 1905, the Russian and Japanese Navies met in the Battle of Tsushima Island, Japan. Always proud of their military prowess, Russia sent a massive fleet. What they didn't know, however, was the Japanese Navy used better ships that moved with greater speeds than the Russian ships. The Japanese had better tactics and a more advanced telegraph system that penetrated the heavy fog conditions which set in the morning of the battle, all but blinding the light flashing & flag-waving of the Russian communications. They lost 28 ships in the battle to only three of the Japanese torpedo boats, forcing the Russians to flee in defeat.

Pumped with arrogant pride over their insidious assault on the American Navy in Pearl Harbor, the Japanese thought the Battle of Midway would be their crowning sequel to the Hawaiian attack. They planned to draw the American fleet into an ambush, slam them with additional forces and destroy what was left of our carrier and capital fleet. Instead, America captured Japanese communications traffic and set an ambush of their own.

Japan was working on the assumption America would only have two carriers and a demoralized, weakened Navy. The United States Navy showed up on June 4, 1942, with an extra carrier putting over 120 more planes in the air, vastly outnumbering Japan, who lost three carriers and almost 250 aircraft. The battle tipped the scales and shifted power in the Pacific during World War II.[24]

In both battles, the defeated countries assumed things about their enemies which were underestimated or erroneous. They encountered elements about their opposition they were not aware of. This lack of knowledge served their defeat and made their enemies the victors. Especially in spiritual warfare against the enemies of darkness, we must know the tactics and capabilities of Satan and his vast force of demonic spirits, lest we suffer the loss of various battles even though in the end, believers in Christ know we win the war.

We have now defined the established system of Satan's diabolical network and at least four basic strategies adopted as their tactical objectives. The next chapter will define some general schemes employed to engage those strategies in our world.

---

[24] Logan Nye, *7 worst military defeats in modern history,* January 2, 2022, We Are the Mighty, www.wearethemighty.com.

CHAPTER THREE

THE DIABOLICAL NETWORK OF EVIL: THE SCHEMES EMPLOYED

Detective Duane Foutch of the Waterloo, Iowa Police Department was our brother-in-law, married to Carol's sister, Karen. We lost him to lung cancer in May 1992, at the young age of just 47. Duane was an excellent investigator who poured himself into his work and earned various professional recognitions for his skill and success in criminal forensics. He was highly respected among his colleagues, who made a commanding presence at his funeral services. Attired in full uniform, a complete section of the church was reserved for the dozens of city, county, and state law enforcement officers with whom he closely served. I remember looking out the back window of our vehicle as we processed to the cemetery and seeing a line of patrol units with flashing lights extending more than a mile behind the family cars. It was an awe-inspiring display of love and support to our family while expressing a great moment of honor and respect for their comrade.

Being a decorated law enforcement officer held significant meaning for Duane, but that wasn't his spirit and passion. He was an avid sportsman, especially when it came to fishing. I'm not talking about just a great hobby; Duane could have produced his own professional television sporting series for how to go after the big ones! He was that good!

Many times, when our family was gathered, we found ourselves in a boat somewhere with Duane doing what he loved most to do. On one occasion, Duane and I were heading out for a trip to Minnesota near where the mighty Mississippi River begins. In the early spring of the year, the ice-covered waters began to break up from the sub-zero temperatures common in the north. He maneuvered his metal boat slowly around chunks of ice as big as automobiles! You would never put a fiberglass bass boat in those waters, and I learned you don't wear tennis shoes with thin socks in a metal boat trolling over near-freezing waters either!

In preparation for this one-day fishing excursion, I followed Duane down into his basement to collect our gear. There were military-style chests organized around the basement, which held his fishing equipment. One chest was labeled a "bass" chest (different sections for large-mouth and small-mouth); another, a "walleye" chest; another, a great northern "pike" chest; and yet another, a "crappie" chest! This guy was serious! He had amassed thousands of dollars in fishing lures, rods & reels, and other equipment invested to maximize his great passion for "wetting a line."

Watching this man fish was like observing the work of a fine artist in action. A sportsman of this rank would never climb in the boat with just one pole. Duane had a half-dozen rods & reels, all rigged with different bait and lure set-ups. He would stop in the bait shop and inquire among the locals "what they were hitting on." His boat served as my first introduction in the late-1970s to electronic depth finders. This was not just a relaxing day on the water; this man was after fish!

Duane would pull into a cove or inlet of the lake which had a "promising look," cast one rig out, and play it a bit around the bank, near stumps, foliage, etc. If nothing "hit on" that particular rig, he would reel it in and cast another. He played top bait, shallow-water lures, spinnerbaits, some yellow, some green, others silver which sparkled with sun reflection – all in a strategic effort to see what they were hitting on. He didn't waste much time with the no-hitters, but once he felt the familiar bump on the line, he knew he had their attention.

Do you think Duane put that rig up and pulled out another one to try? Not on your life! He now knew what spurred their reaction, so he worked it with even more intensity. You could see the change in his demeanor. Focus, intent, and fierce determination took over. Duane was going to get that fish, and he didn't stop with all his strategy and schemes until the fish grabbed the bait and he jerked back on the pole setting the hook. Reeling in the prize, that fish was history…and dinner later that night!

While I would never characterize Duane as being sinister, Satan and his forces of evil operate with similar tactics and tenacity. The Apostle Paul instructs us to *put on the full armor of God, that we may be able to stand firm against the schemes of the devil* (Ephesians 6:11). The Greek word Paul uses for *schemes* is METHODEIA, where we get our English word, method. It is a compound word referring to the process of lying-in wait to trick someone. It is very cunning and deceitful, yet crafty and sharp.

We noted the first place Satan showed up after being cast down to the earth from heaven was in the Garden of Eden, embodying an ancient reptile form described as *more crafty than any beast of the field* (Genesis 3:1). The Hebrew word translated *crafty* is similar in meaning to the Greek word for *schemes*. It means cunning and shrewd, yet sensible and convincing. Satan is not as dumb as we often think him to be. He is far more intelligent than most realize, but only in evil, diabolical ways. The methods and tactics he can develop and orchestrate among his forces of darkness are not to be taken lightly or for granted.

Paul also tells us to *take up the shield of faith with which you will be able to extinguish all the flaming missiles of the evil one* (Ephesians 6:16). When the Persians invaded Athens, Greece, in 480 B.C., they used arrows wrapped with flammable plant fibers dipped in pitch (tar material) and set aflame. These aerial projectiles were highly effective in burning down wooden barricades used to fortify battalions of troops or a small city.[25]

Our nation has been inundated since 2020 with racial protests targeted at police brutality, incited from the death of George Floyd at the hands of Minneapolis ex-police officer Derek Chauvin who was later convicted on three counts of murder and manslaughter in the case. The "Black Lives Matter" and ANTIFA movements staged what liberal politicians and mainstream media kept insisting were "peaceful protests." However, destroying property, burning down

---

[25] Weapons and Warfare, History and Hardware of Warfare, *The First Incendiary Missiles,* March 28, 2017, www.weaponsandwarfare.com.

buildings, looting, stealing, and injuring & killing human beings is a far cry from peace! These tactics and schemes are defined and developed straight out of hell!

As a teenager growing up in Memphis, Tennessee, during the 60s, Dr. Martin Luther King was traveling the nation speaking out on civil rights, and similar protests with savage rioting broke out across our country. That was when I first learned about "Molotov cocktails," a homemade incendiary device consisting of a glass bottle filled with flammable liquid, lit, and hurled through the air into a waiting target. It got its name from Vyacheslav Molotov, a Russian diplomat who developed similar grenades during World War II.

We have seen a re-introduction of the Molotov cocktail during these "peaceful protests" of our day. If you think these flaming projectiles are mere modern coincidence, you would be vastly underestimating the tactical schemes of outer darkness. There is no reason not to assume Paul addresses both a symbolic and a literal weapon of spiritual warfare when he designates *flaming missiles*. Jesus prophesied that during these last days, *kingdoms will be rising up against kingdoms* (Matthew 24:7) as *lawlessness increases* (Matthew 24:12). The civil unrest and racial hostilities developing among our countrymen serve as a vivid manifestation of the acts of war being instigated in the portals of hell and a glaring reminder, we are in the closing days of the Church Age.

As we look more closely at the various schemes of Satan's diabolical network, we note three common ones.

Schemes of Appraisal

James offers great insight into the development of sinful choices and their devastating effect – *Let no man say when he is tempted, "I am being tempted by God;" for God cannot be tempted by evil, and He Himself does not tempt anyone. But each one is tempted when he is carried away and enticed by his own lust. Then when lust has conceived, it gives birth to sin; and when sin is accomplished, it brings death* (James 1:13-15). Before we break this principle down further, please note the last phrase, *it brings death*. Remember what death is? Part of Satan's rudimentary strategies – *kill, steal, and destroy*! A strategy can be seen as an objective, and a scheme serves as a tactic developed to meet that objective.

We are prone to feel the heat of the battle in spiritual warfare when we fall under the temptation to sin and a need to place the blame for why we are. Some want to credit the temptation to God, but James makes it very clear in this passage God cannot and does not tempt anyone to sin. The proverbial angel on one shoulder and the devil on the other is said to make us decide whether God is to blame, or the devil is the culprit.

When I was a teenager, one of the popular comedians was Flip Wilson, whose claim to fame was the punch line, "the devil made me do it." Flip made millions off that one famous line. Let me ask you a question. Did Satan rattle his tail, open wide his mouth, stick out his venomous fangs and make Eve take a bite of that fruit else she would be bitten and suffer a grueling death? Of course not. When you spoke those words of profanity, did Satan take over your mouth, tongue, and vocal cords causing you to speak curse words involuntarily? When you surfed over to those pornographic websites, did Satan seize your hand, arm, and eyes and force you involuntarily to move your mouse, click and indulge in those graphic images?

James is helping us place blame where the blame should properly be placed. When we sin, it is neither God's nor the devil's fault. The responsibility lies with you and me – *WE are carried away and enticed by OUR OWN lust.* We have no one to blame but ourselves. We choose sinful behavior. No one makes us do so; we make a willing and voluntary choice ourselves to sin.

Notice James reveals our lust is *conceived.* The Greek word means to capture or arrest. When a woman conceives, a sperm seizes and captures an egg, fertilizing it with the miracle of life. The word can also mean seizing oneself as a prisoner to his own passions and lusts in a hostile sense.

Where does our propensity to sin come from? Fundamentally, it comes from that big mistake of Eve and Adam back in the Garden of Eden. We call it the "fall of man." Paul explains, *just as through one man sin entered into the world, and death through sin, and so death spread to all men because all sinned* (Romans 5:12). It is inherent throughout all humanity from every generation of Adam, all the way to you, me, mine, and yours. We don't have to be taught how to sin; it is already a part of our fallen human nature straight from birth.

The Book of Romans is rich in the doctrine and theology of our Christian faith. Paul clarifies *while we were in the flesh, the sinful passions...were at work in the members of our body to bear fruit for death* (7:5). Regarding our fleshly nature, Paul says, *I am of flesh, sold into bondage to sin* (7:14). He admits, *I know nothing good dwells in me, that is, in my flesh; for the willing is present in me, but the doing of the good is not* (7:18). He describes the great spiritual battle between our Godly spiritual nature and our unspiritual fleshly nature. We can all relate!

Additionally, our propensity to sin comes from our hearts and mind. God spoke through the Old Testament prophet Jeremiah to remind us our *heart is more deceitful than all else and is desperately sick* (Jeremiah 17:9). Paul explains – *For those who are according to the flesh set their minds on the things of the flesh, but those who are according to the Spirit set their minds on the things of the Spirit. For the mind set on the flesh is death, but the mind set on the Spirit is life and peace; because the mind set on the flesh is hostile toward God...and those who are in the flesh cannot please God* (Romans 8:5-8). Our hearts and minds are the sources of our sinful behavior. These are the places within us where sin is inherently conceived, and the blame for our sinful choices lies. We choose to set our minds on one or the other.

I began this chapter talking about my late brother-in-law, Duane because his fishing methods remind me of this great insight of James. In this passage, two Greek words are actual fishing terms - *enticed and carried away*. The first means to catch by bait, while the second means to lure and draw out to be seized and captured, or as we would say, "swallow hook, line, and sinker."

Peter lets us know *our adversary, the devil, prowls about like a roaring lion, seeking someone to devour* (I Peter 5:8). See it like Satan is on a fishing expedition. He wants to make a catch so he can devour his produce. Why is Satan prowling, lurking, seeking?

Because the rudimentary strategy of his system is to kill, steal and destroy. He can violently & directly attack, but his most effective means is to lure you into loss, destruction, and death, by whatever means he can. But how does he know the most effective means for any given person? How does he know what bait to use, where and when to cast it?

To get the full impact of these thoughts, we must consider three divine attributes of God and how Satan measures against them. I cannot find any place in Scripture where Satan is depicted as having any of these three attributes:

Omnipresence

God is present everywhere, at all times, past-present-future. That is a complex reality for us to fully understand. Still, it speaks to the infinite quality of God as His presence spans eternity past, eternity present, and eternity future simultaneously. It is a great comfort to know God's presence always surrounds us throughout our lives.

Satan, on the other hand, is NOT omnipresent. He cannot be everywhere, at all times, past-present-future. He can only be in one place at one time. Don't forget a third of the angels of heaven were cast down to the earth with him, so he has millions of demonic beings widely scattered across our world doing his bidding. But, like Satan, they can only be in one place at a time. Because of their number, however, there is hardly a moment or an area when dozens of them are not lurking and observing.

Omnipotence

God is all-powerful. The Scripture assures us *all things are possible with God* (Matthew 19:26), and absolutely *nothing is impossible with God* (Luke 1:37), illustrated through the miraculous virgin birth and bodily resurrection of Jesus Christ. Because God is all-powerful, there is nothing God cannot do.

Satan has limited & temporary supernatural powers far beyond what most people might imagine, but he is NOT all-powerful. It cannot be said of Satan that all things are possible with him, and nothing is impossible for him. His power, be what it may, is still drastically limited compared to God.

Omniscience

God is all-knowing. God always knows everything, past-present-future simultaneously. In this way, God is exactly like His omnipresence. He is always everywhere, and He always knows everything. What a great comfort! The revealing words of the Psalmist speak to this reality – *Your eyes have seen my unformed substance; and in Your book were all written all the days that were ordained for me, when as yet there was not one of them* (Psalm 139:16).

I find it unreasonable not to trust my life to the only One who knows every detail of the present and every minute of my future. Nothing takes God by surprise. He is never blindsided. I cannot see around the next corner and what may be coming at me over the next hill, but God can, and He already knows the outcome. If I can walk throughout life with this kind of felt assurance, I can live confidently in His omniscient and omnipotent care.

The Bible also assures us God *searches me and knows me...understands my thoughts* (Psalm 139:1-2). Nowhere in Scripture can I find where Satan has this ability. People will often say, "Satan put this thought in my mind...." I cannot find a Biblical reference to suggest this is accurate or supernaturally possible for Satan. Satan is NOT omniscient. He cannot read your mind, nor can he place an evil thought in your mind. Remember, our evil thoughts come from our deceitful hearts and sinful, fleshly nature, which influence our minds.

These things being true, how is it then, Satan and his network of evil forces *prowl* and *devour*? This will be a shocking and sobering epiphany for some, but we must understand how this works. Satan cannot always be everywhere, always know everything, nor have unlimited power to process either. The only scheme he can play is to *seek* (I Peter 5:8). The Greek word ZETEO means to inquire and observe for purposes of plotting against.

The only things Satan and his demonic spirits can know & understand about you are what you reveal to them yourself. Pause a moment and let that sink in! They are always lurking around every corner, watching, observing, taking notes, and reporting back to the war room. They see every place you go, every movie you watch, every book you read, and every website you surf. They hear every word which comes out of your mouth and every conversation you have with others. They listen to every expression of your thoughts, opinions, and viewpoints. They are constantly watching, listening, and learning your every weakness and point of vulnerability so they know what flaming missiles they can hurl across the path of your life to hit you in whatever way they can to kill, steal or destroy you.

Because they cannot read your thoughts and can only learn by observation, they go on a fishing expedition with your life. Because they observed you and your spouse arguing over money problems, for instance, they will cast a lure into your waters which baits you to some unethical, unlawful, or otherwise non-productive money scheme, presented in such a way it promises instant and abundant wealth (remember, an angel of light…sheep's clothing). You take the bait, he sets the hook, and you're in bankruptcy and foreclosure before you know it (kill, steal and destroy).

Because they observed you viewing pornography for hours in front of your computer screen, they learned you have a weakness and vulnerability in your sexual integrity. They will cast sensual lures across the path of your life, intending to entice you into illicit & immoral behaviors and relationships. You take the bait in a moment of weakness, and he sets the hook. Your sin is exposed. You are under arrest, terminated from your job, in the divorce court, and treated for some incurable sexually transmitted disease. You face jail time, public shame, perhaps an illegitimate child, and your life is destroyed from one weak moment. You have become the victim of a kill-steal-destroy fishing expedition.

Please understand the effectiveness of this strategy and scheme. Each time the forces of hell hear you say, "I am worried that…;" you have just announced over their loudspeakers precisely what they can bring into your life that will produce stress, anxiety, suffering, and heartache. Each time they hear you say, "I am afraid that…;" you just revealed to them what they could bring into your life to produce significant threat and terror. You can undoubtedly assume whatever that is; it will result in some form of kill, steal, and destroy. Because it is YOU they are listening to and learning from, learn to control your tongue – *it is a restless evil and full of deadly poison* (James 3:8). Don't help the forces of darkness with ideas about how to attack your life! They have enough success just fine on their own!

By this same token, James also tells us our tongue can produce *blessing* (3:9-10). Remember, the demons of hell are always lurking and listening, so let them hear you praising and worshipping your Heavenly Father. Pray out loud, so they hear your prayers. Read Scripture out loud so they can listen to you quoting God's Word. Let them hear you praying for God's protection over the lives of your children, grandchildren, and friends. Let them listen to you pleading with God to subdue their power so *no weapon formed against you (or yours) will prosper* (Isaiah 54:17). Rebuke them out loud and let them hear you pray to God for a wall of protection to surround your life, serving as a fortress against their principalities and powers of darkness. Learn to fight your adversary, the devil, because if you don't, you might be devoured!

Schemes of Accusation

The process we have just described serves another purpose in hell's scheme of things. As Satan and his demon spirits lurk and observe, they are learning our weaknesses & vulnerabilities. Then they hurl flaming missiles across the path of our lives, enticing and engaging us until they entrap us, resulting in our faltering into sin. Now Satan has grounds to enter the courts of God in heaven and accuse us, which John reveals as a fact – *the accuser of our brethren...who accuses them before our God day and night* (Revelation 12:10).

Earlier, we noted an example of this prosecutorial effort of Satan in the life of Job. Another example involves Joshua - *Then he showed me Joshua the high priest standing before the angel of the Lord, and Satan standing at his right hand to accuse him. And the Lord said to Satan, "The Lord rebuke you, Satan!"...now Joshua was clothed in filthy garments and standing before the angel. And he spoke and said to those who were standing before him saying, "Remove the filthy garments from him." Again, he said to him, "See, I have taken your iniquity away from you and will clothe you with festal robes."* (Zechariah 3:1-4). This vision was extended to the prophet Zechariah to illustrate the basic message God wanted him to proclaim to the idolatrous people of Israel – *The Lord was very angry with your father. Therefore, say to them, "Thus says the Lord of hosts, 'Return to Me,' declares the Lord of hosts, 'that I may return to you,' says the Lord of hosts."* (Zechariah 1:2-3).

Fortunately, I have not had to enter a courtroom many times in life. Yes, for a few vehicle violations over the years, and working with a national organization called Court-Appointed Special Advocates (CASA) for Children as an observer to our work. I have noted that the same primary players are commonly present in the courtroom.

The heavenly court Zechariah describes has corresponding officials to our earthy courts.

God (Judge)

The Psalmist declares *God Himself is judge* (50:6)...*God is the judge; He puts down one and exalts another* (75:7). God is the Judge because He is the only one credible to judge – *God is a righteous*

Judge (7:11). Only God is qualified to sit on the heavenly bench and execute righteous justice. The Supreme Court of heaven is the highest, and God Himself is the Supreme Chief Justice.

Satan (Prosecutor)

Through the writings of Zechariah, Job, and Revelation, we have already identified the Prosecutor as Satan, the one who accuses.

You (Defendant)

You and I are the ones who stand accused, simply because we are all under sin – *For all have sinned and come short of the glory of God* (Romans 3:23)...*there is none righteous, not even one* (3:10)...*if we say that we have no sin, we are deceiving ourselves, and the truth is not in us* (I John 1:8). Many have been arrested & charged with crimes they did not commit, so their hope is the judicial process will prove and declare their innocence. The problem with you and me in this heavenly court is we have no such plea. We are clearly & blatantly guilty without excuse, placing us entirely at the mercy of the court.

Word (Law & Jury)

David pleaded in the Psalm – *Judge me, O Lord my God, according to Thy righteousness* (35:24). God hears our case and hands down His decision based on the righteousness of His Word – *For the Word of God is living and active and sharper than any two-edged sword, and piercing as far as the division of soul and spirit, of both joints and marrow, and able to judge the thoughts and intentions of the heart* (the inherent parts of our sinful nature). *And there is no creature hidden from His sight, but all things are open and laid bare to the eyes of Him with whom we have to do* (Hebrews 4:12-13). God sees all and knows all, and we stand before His court accused for how we have failed to measure up against the holy, righteous standard of His Word. Its precepts, laws, and commands define our violations, declare our verdict of guilt, and dictate the terms of our sentence.

Cross (Exoneration)

It seems each time a politician, corporate officer, entertainer, or some other well-known person is arrested and charged; they are often heard to say on the news, "I look forward to my day in court where I am fully confident, I will be completely exonerated of all these accusations." That is the hope of anyone sitting at the defendant's table, but as we know, it is not the way things always turn out. Our modern judicial processes are prejudiced too much with legal technicalities, the shifting shades of "reasonable doubt," and the artistic talents of expensive attorneys who know just the right way to present the facts in a case, so they tilt in favor of their clients. As a result, genuinely guilty criminals often walk free, and genuinely innocent victims go to prison, corrupting justice along the way.

There is only one hope of exoneration in this heavenly court, and it comes only through the redemptive work Jesus Christ accomplished on the cross. As we have said, our guilt is already established – *for all have sinned and come short of the glory of God* (Romans 3:23). The truth which cannot be denied follows that declaration – *the wages of sin is death* (Romans 6:23). Surely Satan knew when he lied to Eve in the garden that her disobedience to

God's command would indeed result in death. Even if he didn't, now that death is the penalty for sin, Satan comes to the heavenly court accusing us of sin and seeking the death penalty for our guilt, his most rudimentary goal.

Whether or not Satan understood the plan of God for the work of the cross back there in the Garden, what was accomplished on Calvary's hill was more complete than Satan realized. Paul reminds us that Jesus, *being found in appearance as a man, humbled Himself by becoming obedient to the point of death, even death on a cross* (Philippians 2:8). This act of sacrifice accomplished a substitutionary result – *having canceled out the certificate of debt consisting of decrees against us, which was hostile to us; and He has taken it out of the way, having nailed it to the cross* (Colossians 2:14). The *certificate of debt* to which Paul refers is the hostile death penalty for sin decreed against us.

When I was a senior in high school, I met all the credits necessary for graduation, leaving me with a two-hour study hall at the end of each day. The Memphis City School system had a policy enabling such students to acquire a work permit and leave school for their job. I had landed a job as a disc jockey for a local Christian radio station. One afternoon, I was running late and, in my rush, maneuvered an intersection to avoid a traffic jam up ahead. In doing so, I carelessly made an illegal U-turn and ran a red stop sign which I thought was simply a yellow yield sign. One of the oncoming vehicles just happened to be a Memphis Police unit! He pulled me over and wrote me a citation for both violations. There was no question about my guilt or deliberation about the fine since the municipal law dictated what I would have to pay - $39, which was a considerable price tag for a 16-year-old in 1973.

To illustrate this substitutionary result, let me pose an extended scenario. Suppose while I was on the side of the road with that police officer, a stranger happened by and observed the situation. He pulled over, came to where the officer and I were standing, and after a brief conversation, offered, "Please give me this young man's citation and let him go free. I will pay his fine." The officer shrugged, gave the stranger my citation, and we all drove away.

This is essentially what Jesus Christ did on the cross. He paid our citation (certificate of debt - death). He took it out of the way and nailed it to the cross – *He Himself bore our sins in His body on the cross, so that we might die to sin and live to righteousness* (I Peter 2:24).

I wish I could say the full effect of this substitutionary death was automatically applied to all human life, but I can't because it is not. Today, many in our world believe that when you die, you automatically go to heaven to be with God. Jesus made it undeniably clear this is not the case when He told Nicodemus *unless one is born again, he cannot see the kingdom of God* (John 3:3). It is certainly an effect available to you, but it is something you must initiate through faith in Christ (go back and read through the previous discussion on the "faith" word, PISTEWO). We are only born again when we place our faith in Christ, and it is only with that commitment that the substitutionary effect of the cross is applied to our life.

Another significant effect is also applied which exonerates us in the heavenly court. In theological and doctrinal terms, we call it "justification." This amazing effect is when the blood of Jesus is applied to the sins of our life because of our faith commitment to

Him. When God looks at our life, rather than see the guilt of our sin, He only sees the shed blood of His Son covering our sin – *all things are cleansed with blood, and without shedding of blood there is no forgiveness* (Hebrews 9:22). Accordingly, God justifies us as holy and righteous and declares us innocent even when we are not! How? Only by the shed blood of Jesus on the cross applied to our life through faith, and by God's rich mercy and grace – *there is therefore now no condemnation for those who are in Christ Jesus* (Romans 8:1). We all want to be exonerated when guilty, and especially when innocent. What Jesus accomplished for us on the cross is the only lawful avenue by which such mercy can be applied in the heavenly court.

Jesus (Defense Attorney)

When we are compelled to go to court, we want the best attorney we can afford to represent us. We have a court-appointed defender who is the absolute best in the heavenly court! His name is Jesus Christ. When we surrender our heart and life to Him as our personal Savior and Lord, He represents us before His heavenly Father when Satan stands to accuse us.

So, the proceedings might sound something like this:

Satan – "Your Honor, comes the Prosecution with charges of unrighteous conduct on the part of the accused, Rick Smith."

God – "Mr. Smith, how do you plead?"

Accused – "Your Honor, I am shamefully guilty as charged."

Satan – "The prosecution rests, Your Honor! He has admitted his guilt, and the Law declares he should be put to death. I move, therefore, for an immediate sentence of death."

God – "Not so fast, Mr. Prosecutor. Is there any word from the Defense?"

Jesus – "Yes, Your Honor. The defense would like to submit for evidence this exhibit, a copy of page 967,630,739 of the Book of Life recorded on September 11, 1963, showing an entry of Mr. Smith's name upon his confession of faith in Your Son. Based on this exculpatory evidence, I move to dismiss all charges against My client."

Satan – "Objection, Your Honor! The defense is prejudiced because He is Your Son. This is a clear conflict of interest. I demand He recuse Himself from these proceedings immediately! The accused has already admitted his unquestionable guilt! Put him to death!"

God – "Objection over-ruled! I will now hear closing arguments, beginning with the Prosecution."

Satan – "Your Honor, this man is evil, vile, and wretched. He is a sinister hypocrite underneath all those spiritual good looks on the outside. He doesn't deserve Your mercy or leniency. He deserves to die in his shame, guilt, and humiliation. Your Law states He must die because of his sin, and I adjure the court to render the only just verdict and sentence in this case – death!"

Jesus – "Your Honor, it is true My client is guilty as charged. Indeed, he doesn't deserve Your grace and mercy, nor Your leniency as the Prosecutor has so gleefully pointed out. However, Your Honor, based upon his profession of faith in Me as His Savior & Lord, his condemnation was nullified, and My completed work on the cross redeemed his life. Therefore, he has been justified holy by My blood, and his sin debt has been eternally canceled. He has confessed his sin and based on the authority and promises of Your Word, I move for immediate dismissal of all charges, so Mr. Smith can stand forgiven and reconciled back in full fellowship with Your Honor."

God – "So be it! Case dismissed. You are free, Mr. Smith. I do not condemn you, sir; go and sin no more."

Someone once said grace is God giving us what we don't deserve, and mercy is God NOT giving us what we DO deserve. This is beautifully true when it comes to the sin in our lives. When we stand accused of sin, we are guilty as charged. But at that moment, we have an advocate with God – *if we confess our sins, He is faithful and righteous to forgive us our sins and to cleanse us from all unrighteousness* (I John 1:9). When that happens, *as far as the east is from the west, so far has He removed our transgressions from us* (Psalm 103:12). Just how far is that?

If you were to begin walking in a northerly direction, eventually, you would come to the place at the North Pole where all the earth's longitudes meet at one point. The instant you step over that point, you will have ceased walking north and began walking south. When you cross the same point at the South Pole, you will start walking north again. North and south have beginning and ending points at each pole of our planet. There is no infinity in their directions.

It is very different, however, with east and west. If you start walking in an easterly direction, you will never cross a point anywhere on the earth when you have ceased walking east and begin walking west. At the same time, if you start walking in a westerly direction, you will never come to a point where you cease walking west and begin walking east. We have then an illustration of infinity. When God forgives us of our sin, He removes it *as far as east is from west* - to a place of infinity where it can never be retrieved.

If that weren't enough, the Scripture further reveals God *wipes out our transgressions for (His) own sake; and I will not remember your sins* (Isaiah 43:25). Get the full impact of this statement. Remember, one of the divine attributes of God is His omniscience; that is, He is all-knowing. He knows everything, all the time, past-present-future, simultaneously. So, we could say God can't forget anything, including our sin.

The beautiful and merciful thought in this promise is God may still know about my sin, but He chooses not to hold it in his thinking cap against me. The Hebrew word for *remember* is ZARKAR, which means to recount or bring back to mind. In other words, very unlike you and me, God doesn't hold a "gunny sack." When we sin (again) and come to God in confession pleading for forgiveness, He doesn't reach into His gunny sack, pull out our previous violation and say, "No, you committed that same sin last Friday and ten times the month before, and here you are begging its pardon once again." God chooses not to ever hold up a previous, forgiven sin to us again.

He remembers it no more and removes it to an infinite place where He never intends to retrieve it.

Let me say just a word about confession before we move on. John's promise of our cleansing from unrighteousness is based on our confession (I John 1:9). The Greek word translated *confess* is HOMOLOGEO. The root prefix is HOMO, meaning the same. The root suffix is LOGOS, referring to a spoken word. Together they mean to speak the same word or to have the same mind. Confession, therefore, is agreeing with God about our sin. If God's Word says something is sin and that sinful behavior has been identified as part of our lives, we agree with God that it is indeed sin. We don't argue about it, make excuses for it, or try and justify it somehow; we agree with God that this is sin in my life. It's not just getting caught and having to admit something; it is an honest and humble agreement with God.

Wow! All of this is good stuff when it comes to being accused before God by our enemy, the devil, which happens all the time, *day and night* (Revelation 12:10). When we go into the heavenly court, we go in with a strong case! We are pardoned before we are ever tried! What human criminal court offers that kind of benefit? You can pause here and have another glory shout…I sure am!

We are defining the schemes of Satan's diabolical network of evil. We have discussed schemes of appraisal and schemes of accusation. We move on to the final basic scheme.

Schemes of Aversion

Although rich in the divine revelation of New Testament Scripture, the essence of Paul's ministry was preaching the Gospel to the Gentile (non-Jewish) world. He encountered many pagan nations and people groups in that effort across the ancient Middle East and Asia Minor. Fortunately, many were open to the Gospel, and Paul and others started churches throughout these areas. He also met resistance and persecution. Many seemed distracted, and their attention diverted away from his message. Paul was discerning enough to understand this resistance was more than just cultural, religious, or political; it was diabolical.

In writing to the church at Corinth, he said, *if our gospel is veiled, it is veiled to those who are perishing, in whose case the god of this world (Satan) has blinded the minds of the unbelieving, that they might not see the light of the gospel of the glory of Christ* (II Corinthians 4:3-4). The Greek word translated *blinded* refers to making obscure, opaque, or cloudy. Our *mind*, of course, is the place of our perception, perspectives, and our ability to think, rationalize and process information.

The sinister revelation Paul is giving here alerts us to Satan's ability to use outward dynamics to cloud people's thinking, obscure their perspectives, and *veil* (cover or conceal) their understanding of themselves as lost persons in need of the saving Gospel of Jesus Christ. Satan accomplishes this through diversion, distraction, and distortion; basically, anything to shift the mind and attention of a person away from hearing the Gospel message. Satan, no doubt, knows *faith comes from hearing and hearing by the word of Christ*

(Romans 10:17). So, he does all he can to make sure the hearing of lost persons is diverted from the Gospel message.

Earlier, we cited an example of Paul's experience when sharing the Gospel with the Proconsul, Sergius Paulus (Acts 13:6-12). We also touched on this same scheme as it played out in Jesus' teaching in the Parable of the Sower (Matthew 13:3-8; 18-23). The heartbreaking reality is Satan already has the lost people of this world, and all he must do is work to keep them. Satan wants no one to spend eternity in heaven with God. Why would he? That is where he was exiled from, so it is the last place he wants anyone to be. He would rather have all men and women spend eternity with him in the Lake of Fire. So, his aversion strategies serve this purpose.

In averting lost people away from the Gospel, Satan is essentially launching an attack upon the Great Commission of the church, which he has done from its inception. The property Ananias and Sapphira agreed to sell and give the proceeds to the early church illustrate Satan's earlier attacks on the church. The couple held back a portion of the money they had committed – *But Peter said, "Ananias, why has Satan filled your heart to lie to the Holy Spirit, and to keep back some of the price of the land?"* (Acts 5:3). Both instantly died because of their sin (Satan's ultimate strategy – kill).

Peter once challenged Jesus when He told His disciples He *must go to Jerusalem and suffer many things from the elders and chief priests and scribes, and be killed, and be raised up on the third day* (Matthew 16:21). That would not be the only time Jesus announced this plan of God to them. It always amazes me how it seemed they never heard another word after *and be killed.* It was such a preposterous thought, they tuned out every word following it, including the best part - *and be raised on the third day*. Perhaps it is why they were so devastated when Jesus was finally crucified and so shocked when they saw Him miraculously resurrected, just like He said He would be!

Peter couldn't bear the thought of His Lord being killed, so he blurted out, *"God forbid it, Lord! This shall never happen to You!"* (16:22), to which Jesus quickly turned and rebuked Peter saying, *"Get behind Me, Satan! You are a stumbling block to Me; for you are not setting your mind on God's interests, but man's!"* (16:23). Now, Jesus was not directly calling Peter Satan.

Just a few verses prior, Jesus had asked these men, *"Who do people say that the Son of man is?" And they said, "Some say John the Baptist; and others, Elijah; but still others, Jeremiah, or one of the prophets." He said to them, "But who do you say that I am?"* (16:13-15). Who is Jesus to you? I hope you realize in terms of your eternity it matters nothing at all what other people think about Jesus; it only matters what YOU think. Who do YOU say Jesus is? Today, many in our world see Him no differently than those in His day. That is, He is just a name in literature, a character in history, an intelligent teacher, a keen prophet, or just someone who went about doing good for people. But is that all He was?

Peter nailed it when he declared, *Thou art the Christ, the son of the living God* (16:16). Everything a person can wholly and accurately proclaim about Jesus is wrapped up in this one statement. He is the One and only true Son of God, the promised Messiah of heaven. This is the essential thing about Jesus everyone must believe to make a personal commitment of their heart and life to Him as Savior & Lord. Jesus affirmed Peter's great spiritual insight when

He said, *"Blessed are you, Simon Barjona because flesh and blood did not reveal this to you, but My Father who is in heaven."* (16:17). You don't get this kind of knowledge and understanding about Christ from degree programs and institutions of learning; this insight only comes through divine revelation into a person's spirit by faith.

The following statement Jesus makes is so compelling, especially as it relates to the theme of this writing – *"Upon this rock, I will build My church, and the gates of Hades shall not overpower it."* (16:18). Satan may undoubtedly come against the Great Commission of God and the church's ministry in proclaiming the Gospel and bringing lost souls into the Kingdom of God, but he will never defeat the church! The church still stands! Even when preachers fall, the church still stands. Even when governments come against us to reduce our free expression of religion, the church still stands. Satan and his diabolical network of evil will never prevail against the church…never, no, not ever!

So, in one moment, Jesus is praising Peter for having proclaimed such a divinely revealed truth, and in the next, rebuking him for speaking the mission and war strategy of hell! How can such inconsistency come out of a faithful follower of Jesus? James tells us very clearly - *the tongue is a small part of the body, and yet it boasts of great things. See how great a forest is set aflame by such a small fire! And the tongue is a fire, the very world of iniquity; the tongue is set among our members as that which defiles the entire body, and sets on fire the course of our life, and is set on fire by hell…but no one can tame the tongue; it is a restless evil and full of deadly poison. With it, we bless our Lord and Father, and with it, we curse men, who have been made in the likeness of God; from the same mouth come both blessing and cursing. My brethren, these things ought not to be this way* (James 3:5-10)…and multitudes of demon spirits are always lurking and listening to every word!

Let's don't be too hard on Peter. We are so prone to be just as guilty. We, too, can mindlessly speak the language of hell if we are not careful with our raw emotions, rash thoughts, and reactionary words as Peter did on this occasion. Without even being aware of it, Peter declared the mission of Satan's diabolical network to sabotage the church and its growth. If Jesus didn't die, redemption couldn't come. This demonic thought is what Jesus rebuked, not His beloved disciple. I'm sure Peter never forgot the exchange.

One of the most significant attacks Satan has waged on the church in our modern-day has been during the COVID-19 pandemic of 2020. Many churches were forced to suspend their public gatherings of worship in various pockets across our nation and world. Many refused and continued to meet under the religious freedom protection right provided in the First Amendment of the U.S. Constitution. Some of those had civil orders issued against them, some were fined large amounts of money for ignoring those orders, and a few ministers were even temporarily taken into custody. We never thought we would see those kinds of restraints and hostilities against the churches of a free America. If Satan's diabolical network of evil has its way, churches will close worldwide, and Christians will be forced to meet "underground" as they already do in various Third World and Communist countries. It may not happen until the Antichrist comes to power, but the day is coming. The 2020 pandemic put the world in a dress rehearsal for that dreaded day!

Duane was one of those special classes of fishermen who was obsessive-compulsive about his sport. If you accompanied him on a fishing excursion, you would be prepared to leave before daybreak and return after nightfall. No distance was too far if the catch offered great potential. Over the years, he must have invested large sums of money in equipment to maximize his trade. Tenacity would describe such a dedicated fisherman. I drive past a lake on my way to work each day, and I have seen people like Duane fishing in the pouring rain, blowing snow, freezing temperatures, while it is still dark, all night even. They may sit in a boat all day, cooking with a sizzling sunburn and never get a nibble, but they won't give up. They keep working the bait, hoping they finally get the big one, and only reel it in and trailer the boat when they absolutely must.

Such tenacity characterizes the system, strategies, and schemes of hell. Satan and his evil minions just won't quit. They will never give up until they absolutely must. Hatred toward God, wrath toward God's people, and resentment for their final judgment of torment drive them to attack & fight until their last defeat.

CONCLUSION & PREVIEW

To this point in our journey together, we have defined the source, season, separation, surrogates, and standard revealed in our foundational passage – *But the Spirit explicitly says that in the later times some will fall away from the faith, paying attention to deceitful spirits and doctrines of demons* (I Timothy 4:1). We have defined Satan's diabolical network, noting the system in place, the basic strategies which are established, and the typical schemes deployed to engage their evil mission in the world.

In the next volume of this trilogy – *Defining the Doctrines* – we will identify the five fundamental doctrines of this satanic system, authenticate them from their associations in Scripture, and attempt to show how their manifestations are becoming more evident and consequential on the national and international landscape. These are:

The Doctrine of Deity & Dominion

Satan's evil aspiration was to be God and to rule & reign in place of God. That effort of mutiny resulted in his expulsion from Heaven.

Even though he holds limited and temporary dominion as *ruler of this world* (John 12:31) and *prince of the power of the air* (Ephesians 2:2), his aspirations will not fully come to fruition until they are realized during the Tribulation Period. Directly possessed by Satan, the Antichrist will orchestrate a series of sinister events enabling him to take his seat in the Holy of Holies in the Third Temple, declare himself to be God, and command the world to worship him as God. This *abomination of desolation* (Daniel 11:31; Matthew 24:15) will culminate Satan's lustful and tenacious thirst for deity & dominion, albeit short-lived and an ultimate failure.

The militant obsession for power & control among the officials of our government and the political agendas they insist on enforcing are glaring manifestations of this satanic thirst for deity and dominion, paving the way for the future world dictator, the Antichrist.

The Doctrine of Deception

Jesus declared *there is no truth in Satan*, and *he is the father of lies* (John 8:44). Whatever perspective anyone has of Satan must never be void of the simple fact that he and his entire network of evil is deception to the core. It is also highly effective, for they have perfected the art of *disguising themselves as angels of light* (II Corinthians 11:14) and camouflaging their *ravenous* nature with innocent-looking *sheep's clothing* (Matthew 7:15).

The fake news, misinformation, and disinformation permeating the world's social media culture and mainstream news outlets only tip the iceberg of the elaborate measures Satan is orchestrating to promote destructive lies and deception in our nation. It serves to pave the way for his diabolical plan, especially as it lays the foundation for ultimate deception during the coming Tribulation Period.

The Doctrine of Deviation

Moses admonished Joshua and the ancient Israelites to *be careful to do according to all the law...do not turn from it to the right or to the left* (Joshua 1:7). Satan's fundamental strategies serve to lead people astray, deviate from God's Word, will, and ways, reform good into evil and evil into good, and ultimately destroy lives through violation & rebellion against God's divine order. The most apparent manifestation of this radical defiance in our modern culture is the extreme sexual deviation seen in the acceptance & accommodation of LGBT lifestyles, the increase in sex trafficking & pedophilia, cohabitation, infidelity, and sexual promiscuity fueled by the massive proliferation of internet pornography and social network connections. The Bible speaks clearly and directly in condemnation against these perversions and deviations. The truth is not rightly heralded in our current culture until that declaration is courageously made without apology or compromise.

The Doctrine of Division

The religious elite of Jesus' day lamely accused Him of casting out demons by the power of *Beelzebub, the ruler of demons* (Satan) (Matthew 12:24). Jesus revealed a diabolical strategy of darkness when he countered, *"Any kingdom divided against itself is laid waste; and any city or house divided against itself shall not stand."* (12:25). Satan knows this truth all too well, so while he pays careful attention not to let it destroy his kingdom of darkness, he employs this dynamic very effectively in our modern culture.

Racial division has run rampant in American society with the riotous protests of Black Lives Matter (BLM) and ATIFA over social inequalities and police brutality. The "woke culture" is working to eradicate American history and invading our media, entertainment, corporate, industrial, and government sectors, forcing them into compliance with its radical agenda. Never has our nation seen such divisive polarities as currently exist between political parties, the judiciary, and many issues raging at state, county, and municipal levels across our country. It appears we are becoming less and less a "united" federation of states and more of one fracturing into hostile and radically different societies with contrasting agendas and expectations. It all serves as the stage-setting for America to fall easily into the dictatorship of the Tribulation Antichrist.

The Doctrine of Death

When God created mankind in pre-fall Paradise (Eden), He never intended for man ever to know anything about evil, only His goodness & greatness. Satan never wanted humanity to know anything except evil, and the lure to get Adam & Eve to violate God's command and eat from the Tree of the Knowledge of Good & Evil would accomplish that eye-opening awareness. Despite the warning "you shall surely die" if they did, Satan defiantly challenged God's Word with, "you surely shall not die." But the subsequent act of rebellion that followed did indeed usher into the human experience not only the knowledge of evil but also the consequential death (physically & spiritually) associated with it –

the wages of sin is death (Romans 6:23). The fundamental goal of Satan's diabolical network of darkness ever since has been to steal, destroy and KILL. All roads with Satan and his demonic principalities & powers of darkness lead to death. He will take out multiplied millions through sinful choices, and eschatological catastrophes before his biddings are done.

In the next volume, *Defining the Doctrines*, we will explore these elaborate systems of belief & practice and identify how they are permeating, preparing, and propelling our nation and world into the sinister plans of darkness. Some will label those claims as products of religious fanaticism, right-wing fascism, political conspiracies, or otherwise too controversial to consider valid. Nevertheless, I hope you will continue this journey of discovery with me as I strive to present a Biblical explanation for the radical shifts and changes unfolding before our eyes. In doing so, our more profound understanding of the dynamics in this diabolical force can better position us in fighting evil across our land until the sound of the trumpet and the voice of the archangel beckons us to our eternal rendezvous with Jesus in the clouds.

I don't want to close this volume with just an invitation to read the ones to follow. I would be greatly amiss if I didn't offer a different invitation – one that extends to you an opportunity to enter the glorious light of the gospel and the righteous peace of God.

Perhaps as you have read our discussions about PISTEWO (faith) and how belief, commitment, and lifestyle are the necessary elements of walking in a genuine relationship with God through Christ, you have come to realize you have never really made such a commitment. I would invite you to simply bow your heart in repentance and surrender your life to Him.

Your prayer might be as follows: "God, I'm grateful You love me despite all my failures and weaknesses. I'm grateful You understand the struggles I have endured in life, and most of all, I am grateful You allowed Your only Son, Jesus, to die for my sins on the cross. I want to know with full assurance in my heart that You have forgiven me of all my sins, and I ask You to cleanse me from all unrighteousness. From this moment on, I want to commitment my life to You. With Your help, I want to live my life as best I can in obedience to Your Word, will and ways. I ask You to forgive me, save me, and accept me as Your very own. In the name of Your Son, Jesus, I say to You, 'I do.'"

According to the promise of Scripture, anyone who comes sincerely and humbly before God expressing that kind of prayer is graciously saved by the mercy of God. Welcome to the family of faith and to the wonderful gift of eternal life in heaven. I encourage you to find a pastor you know and trust and share with him the experience and commitment you have just made so that he can help guide you in your new walk of faith.

Perhaps this book has opened your eyes to the sobering reality that you have allowed the sinister ploys of darkness to deceive you and lure you into choices, behaviors, and a lifestyle that characterizes and manifests demonic evil. You can be free from those satanic strongholds and surrender your life to God, allowing Him to break those chains that have bound you so tightly and helplessly in their clutches.

Your prayer might be as follows: "God, I want to be free of these evil strongholds that so grip my mind, body & emotions and drive me into lifestyles & relationships that serve my lusts and the evil nature of my flesh. I have struggled so much with shame, guilt, pain, and loss throughout my life. I have allowed Satan and demonic beings to beat me down, beat me up and lure me down paths that have robbed me of everything and everyone I have ever truly loved. They have destroyed my life in so many ways, and if You don't come to me and deliver me from this wickedness, they will surely take my life. I ask You, God, in the name of Jesus Christ, to forgive me, release me, deliver me, and forever fortify my heart and life from their deception and evil ways again. Fill me with Your salvation and Your Holy Spirit and make me greater than all of Satan's power. I thank You that I am free in Jesus' name!"

When you come to God in that kind of genuine desire and passionate plea, it pleases the Father to come to your aid and help you. By the promise of His Word, He does for you what no one else can do nor what you have been unable to do for yourself. I encourage you to pick yourself up, stand strong in the confidence of your forgiveness & deliverance, and walk forward in a newfound freedom found only in the power of God.

But let me warn you, Satan and his minions will not be happy with your defection from their clutches. They will fight you and work fervently to lure you back. You must resist them and stand firm in your faith. Never go back to those things you flirted with that captivated your lusts & desires and led you into their evil ways. Give up those things you did that entangled you in their strongholds. Dive deep into the Word of God, learn His will and ways, and strive with all your heart to walk obediently according to the commands of God.

You need the fellowship of a body of believers to help encourage you, pray for you, hold you accountable and help strengthen your faith. Seek out a local pastor and church that will embrace you and bring you into their loving care. Share your testimony of deliverance and be the example of the holiness & righteousness God has so graciously made you to emulate. The more you draw near to God, the more He will draw near to you; and the more you resist Satan the more he will resist you.

I would love to hear about your journey. You can reach me by email at: templates@suddenlink.com. I am praying for you as you live each moment moving forward in the freedom of Christ. May His blessings enrich and encourage you as you magnify His goodness and greatness as demonstrated in your life.

Volume Two

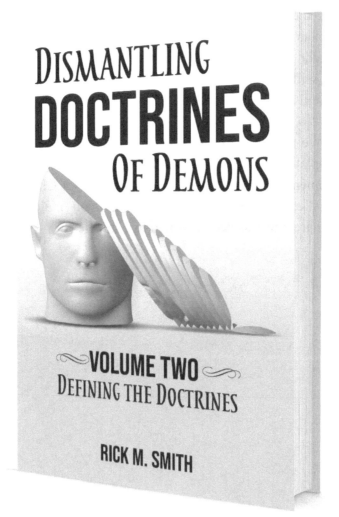

SOON TO BE RELEASED

Made in United States
Troutdale, OR
05/06/2025

31143239R00076